KU-659-061

FIT TO TRAVEL

A light-hearted look at all forms of transport and their funny side – from bike to Boeing, from skates to sea-going liners – join us in the fun and frolics, the memories still so vivid, and the all-round unforgettable moments incurred when people like us travel from A to B.

Also by Tom O'Connor

From the Wood to the Tees
The World's Worst Jokes
One Flew Over the Clubhouse
Take a Funny Turn
Follow Me, I'm Right Behind You

FIT TO TRAVEL

(As from the Liverpool description of a
good-looking girl -

'She's Fit to Travel.')

by

TOM O'CONNOR

First published in Great Britain in 2004
© 2004 Tom O'Connor

The right of Tom O'Connor to be identified as author of this
work has been asserted by him in accordance with the
Copyright, Designs and Patents Act 1988

All rights reserved. No part of this publication may be
reproduced, stored in a retrieval system, or transmitted in any
form or by any means, electronic, mechanical, photocopying,
recording or otherwise, without the prior permission in
writing of the publishers.

Produced for Tom O'Connor by Acer Designs, Manchester
acerdesigns@aol.com
Printed & bound by Ashford Colour Press Ltd., Gosport,
Hampshire

For Faye, Maddi and Amber

You are three bundles of fun and it's great to be
your Grandad

Introduction

Whoever said, "A change is as good as a rest!" has never crossed the Bay of Biscay in a force 10 gale, or spent three days and nights in an airport lounge awaiting the end of an air traffic controller's dispute.

Those documentaries enthusing over the beauties of foreign parts never portray the incidents, accidents and plain misfortunes that can result in travelling there.

All in all, the whole business of travelling is littered with pitfalls and dangers to life, limb and memory bank.

As a seasoned world traveller I've always found the best solution is to discount the hard times and enhance the good times. Laugh and all travellers will laugh with you. Keep an open mind, be prepared for the worst and, perhaps, like me you'll find that getting there is half the fun!

Contents

Chapter 1

The seaside - oh, the seaside!

Maybe, like me, your first recollection of a holiday was a trip to the seaside. Maybe you went by train, or private car if you were well to do. But the chances are your first trip was by coach or, as we used to call it up North, a 'chara'.

Did you have a Mr Pennington who organised the whole event? This included collecting weekly amounts from each family involved in the trip, as well as booking the charabanc or, as Mr Pennington used to call it when he spoke posh, 'the charrow'.

I suppose today Bill Pennington would be hailed as a top drawer travel rep whose devotion to detail was super precise. Every boy and girl, about 30 in all, was supplied with a packed lunch including sandwiches, cakes (all home-made), an apple, an orange and a weird variety of nuts. Along with the usual bottle of 'pop', the parcel for each child included two paper bags; one for the scraps – the other to be sick in!!

The grown-ups who were there to escort us and tend

to our needs would fill the boot of the bus with cases of Guinness and pale ale – 'just in case we don't pass a pub.'

At the duly allotted time we would assemble outside the Olivet Mission in Marsh Lane, Bootle and produce our holiday books – fully stamped and bearing Bill Pennington's initials. Our parents would herd us aboard and give us various warnings about getting lost, getting sunburned ('Rub butter on it if it starts to sting!'), and keeping away from strange men.

Men came no stranger than Bill Pennington. A short, thin man. Thin in every aspect. His frame was very slight, approximately seven stones ringing wet. Five feet six inches that reminded you of a razor blade. The thinnest moustache in the whole free world and the most pronounced limp we'd ever seen. He said he'd been shot in the war and received a gallantry medal. My dad assured us he'd come home drunk one night and been knocked down the stairs by his wife Hilda – eight stones of womanly beauty trapped in a sixteen stone body!

We kids would scramble for control of the huge back seat of the bus but would be driven off with slaps to the back of the head by Hilda - and 'her cohorts, Stella Trubshaw and Elsie Cartwright, together with the latters' husbands Peter and Paul – the Boyle twins. It was hard to say who was the uglier. 'But,' said Stella on many an occasion, 'Better an ugly face than a roving eye.' This would be greeted by a chorus of 'Umm!!' from any ladies in earshot.

So, with General Bill Pennington seated next to the driver and 35 kids sandwiched between him and the phalanx of beauty on the back row, we'd set off for Blackpool leaving a street full of parents outwardly sobbing but inwardly chuckling at their freedom.

Having negotiated the lift bridge at Litherland it became obvious that, with a mixed age range of youngsters, there were going to be bladder problems. The first casualty was 'leak-a-lot Larkin' who never seemed to drink but was never away from a loo! He would spark off a chain reaction and eventually the average speed of the bus was down to about three miles per hour as, one after another, children relieved themselves into gratings along the road to Blackpool.

Also hampering movement was the reaction to Mr Pennington's orders. 'The white paper bag is for your scraps. The brown one is for you to be sick in!'Instantly, every child aboard felt queasy and reached for the bag to heave into. This left a logistical conundrum; was the brown bag full of sick now rubbish to be placed in the white bag?

Complete with all these problems and only a sketchy idea of the route Jim Mitchell, our friendly coach driver, trundled his machine towards Southport and, hopefully, Blackpool whilst chain-smoking Woodbines and whistling 'Galway Bay' through his two remaining teeth. (Central eating my dad used to call him!)

Four hours and several toilet stops later, we would arrive at the coach park near Blackpool Tower, all agog and ready to be overwhelmed by the wonders of the British seaside. But not before a cautionary briefing from 'General Bill'.'Whilst at the seaside do not go near the water!' Blimey! Didn't that contravene the reason we'd gone there in the first place?

'Keep together in groups of four or five and make sure you're all back here at the charrow at five o'clock for fish and chips and lemonade. Then we'll be off home in good time.' He meant good time for the drinking hours of the multitude of pubs we'd passed on the way there.

Somehow, the hours spent near the sea were never as eventful as the time spent on the way there.

Oh yes – we saw the sea, got covered in sand, inside and outside of our clothes, and gained a pinky reddish sunburn on our faces, necks and forearms. None of us ever went brown, except Leo McCarthy who seemed immune to the heat, the flies and the rocking rolling motion of Mr Mitchell's bus. (He should have become an explorer in later years; instead he's a milkman. What a waste!)

We disobeyed orders and paddled in the sea, some of us slipping into the waves and reappearing soaking, shivering and caked in muddy sand. Now came the burning question of the day – would Mr Pennington believe a big boy had pushed us all in??

Accompanied by older kids who kept us together we spent our money on candy floss, rock and hot dogs. (They never taste as good as they smell, do they?) And then, when we thought we could eat not a morsel more, it was five o'clock and we had to return (miraculously with no-one missing) for fish and chips in a newspaper and lemonade to swill it down and help it to swirl round in our innards until queasiness took over.

What a time to feel ill! Tired and overfed. Rumbling along in an undersprung coach at lickety-split speed to reach a good pub - and no sick bag!

Still, the songs we sang kept us cheerful, even whilst abandoned in the pub car park for an hour and a half. Then there was the highlight of the day's entertainment – watching six adults completely plastered – staggering back aboard. Breath like kerosene and eyes rolling!

Obviously they'd quaffed the Guinness and pale ale whilst we'd been at the beach and even Mr Mitchell looked under the weather.

Of course it was before breathalysers and people

always thought they could hold more alcohol than they really should have.

'Drinks like a fish, Jim Mitchell!' Elsie Cartwright would say, 'But it doesn't take a fonk out of him. Wits like razors, eyes like a hawk. He can lip-read in a black-out!' Praise indeed but hardly what was needed when our hero couldn't even lever himself into the driving seat!

'Worry not James,' Bill Pennington assured him. 'Go back and join the ladies and I'll steer us homeward.'

'Good old sobersides,' shrieked Hilda. 'Can't drink too much with his bladder trouble. And it's a godsend on nights like this.'

Secretly, we kids prayed we'd never have bladder trouble – whatever that meant! Particularly since getting drunk meant roaring with laughter and singing bellicose tunes that we kids didn't understand.

Stella Trubshaw, as always, had to sing. She was an unpretty person with a loud voice, who regaled the Jaw Bone Pub on a Saturday night and led the church choir on a Sunday morning through eyes of red and breath of a violent tang. Her favourite song was Saint Theresa of the Roses and, like all good pub singers, began every song with 'Well...'

'Well … Saint Theresa of the roses –er…' (Every line had to end in 'er' so that the song rhymed all the way through.)

Whilst Stella sang, the Boyle twins would accompany her on spoons and bones – both at the wrong tempo.

In this haze of Woodbine smoke, Guinness fumes, and fifth division entertainment, we would arrive home to our 'anxious' (I think not) parents only an hour and a half late. That was good for a Bootle outing. The grown-up 'dos' would sometimes not return till morning. God knows how bad their entertainment was!

Still, the whole experience was good grounding for us kids. We learned lessons which, I'm happy to say, I still draw on today.

Lesson number one was what to take in the way of clothing. Because our elders remembered every summer as being scorchingly hot ('Melted the tarmac, you know. You could fry an egg on the pavement!' my dad would often drone). They would send us off in the flimsiest of outfits. No protection against the elements except a rolled up 'Pacamac' which was of plastic material and kept a lot, but not all, of the rain off.

This was to save us from the odd 'sunshower' but was no help against the biting cold and gale force winds that can sometimes sneak up on you in late afternoon at the British seaside.

If protection against the cold was minimal, protection against the heat was non-existent. Other than the advice to "Rub butter on it if it burns' we had no shield against the rare, but occasionally strong, sunlight of mid-August.

As a consequence we ended up with pink, nay lobster red, skin as taut as a banjo's body and hurting like toothache; forearms, neck, forehead, knees and all exposed parts would plead for help and a knob of butter, even the Co-op's best, did little to oblige.

We were lucky to have thick mops of hair. All except Martin Keenan who was thin of stature, thin of intelligence and, worst of all, thin of hair. Going well on the bald side at twelve years old.

Martin had little other than a knotted handkerchief to cover his exposed cranium, surely the most risky part of the body to be left bare. In later years, armed with Martin's and, in some cases, our own experiences we'd always pack some sort of headgear – even the dreaded school cap!

No thought was given to protective creams for our skin, although the Potter family rubbed themselves in olive oil. To me this seemed to make them pong more and the result of oil and heat from the sun's rays combined seemed to produce a bubbling boiling effect which caused more damage than using nothing.

The fodder we had been provided with was also suspect. Apart from fresh fruit, the rest of the lunch-pack would be large chunks of bread pressed each side of a razor-thin coating of jam, cheese, spam, fish paste – or even condensed milk. A 'conny-onny butty' we used to call it - the size of which was always referred to as a 'door-step'.

Add all these gastronomic delights to fizzy lemonade, or watered down orange juice, seaside rock, candy floss and all manner of unhealthy foods; then top it all off with a portion of greasy undercooked cod and, even greasier, overcooked chips, and you had a mini Mount Vesuvius gurgling inside just waiting for a bumpy bus ride to help it explode.

Then of course, there was the route plan. Never in the history of seaside outings has the entire complement of the bus known where, why and for how long it was going.

All the Bill Penningtons of Christendom combined would never be able to fathom the depths of the British road system. Often road signs were more of a hindrance than a help, particularly those that pointed in the wrong direction because of prevailing wind pressure, or the actions of local tearaways.

No amount of Driver Jim Mitchells could gauge or even guess at the distance, fuel consumption and rough journey time of such a venture. Sometimes the added hazard of garages early closing would enter the equation. It was not unknown for a driver to stop at every garage on the way to top up the bus and every pub on the way back to top up the passengers!!

But of all the salutary lessons we kids would glean from our seaside forays, the one we would remember longest was the choice of fellow travellers. We learned who not to have accompany us, given the choice.

No General Pennington, no blousy Stella and the rhythm of the Boyle twins, no drunken driver, no boring bearers of tales from the 'good old days before you were born, lad.'

No, none of that. Our trips would be self-governed, selected by popular vote, well scouted, well-provisioned and - most importantly - free of dead wood!

This positive thinking produced, in Bootle and possibly where you're from, the kids-only picnic. This could happen anywhere – a village green, a park, someone's back garden, back yard or even a local demolition site. Transport was shanks' pony, but at least it wasn't bumpy. Nor did it require constant checks on petrol, oil levels, tyre pressures or battery acid.

Company was restricted to friends, neighbours, school chums, relatives and anyone else who promised faithfully to be a member of 'our gang', and 'our gang' alone. This gave us a great feeling of camaraderie and allowed us to pooh-pooh any thoughts that we would not be safe or that we would be lured into some form of wrongdoing. No mobile phones in those days but the neighbourhood jungle drums were just as quick with news, if not quite so accurate!

Provisions were an easy item to organise because they literally consisted of anything we personally wanted to eat. Sandwiches, home-made buns, my

Mother's rock cakes ('Guaranteed to kill but not maim,' she used to say, bless her), any amount of sweets, jellies, instant whip (if you don't remember it, ask around) and often highly specialised delights.

We children of Liverpool 20 district had a great affection for cocoa powder mixed with sugar and carried in a paper bag. To taste this exquisite mix needed only one wet forefinger. A dip and a suck and the surge of great bliss could be felt right down to the toes and along the black pumps we wore. (Remember those black pumps? Fit either foot, they did.) You could always tell a kid who had a cocoa bag because he or she could be covered in muck from head to foot but would still always have one pristine forefinger.

To go with our personal eating favourites we obviously needed some form of liquid refreshment. To save time, energy and general hassle, this usually consisted of one large bottle of water or orange squash to be shared between about nine people. Pecking order by size meant that the smallest went last and was left with a bottle full of breadcrumbs and liquid mixed. Added to this was the necessity to prove one was a tough nut by not wiping the top of the bottle after the previous kid. This was a double test of strength if the child before you had that purple ointment on their lips. God knows what you were allowing to enter your nether regions.

Still and all, the picnics were fun. We survived. We became conversant with all kinds of games. The most daring we thought was 'Catch a girl – kiss a girl.' Sadly it was my fate never to be fast enough to catch a good looker. Generally I would end up with Freda Nugent, a notoriously slow runner who was even known to run a little in reverse in order to land the boy she fancied.Still, I felt it was good to be wanted and she was a goodish kisser, despite the teeth braces and thin lips.

How good those memories are. How much fun we seemed to have had. How little stress or strain we felt. If only all journeys and holidays could be like those we remember from so long ago. Okay, they weren't all perfect all the time. There were wet days. There were days we fell out amongst ourselves. There were even times when we vowed 'never again', but in a child's mind never is only until tomorrow and then all is well again. Too bad we can't apply that to today's world. How sad that we can't parcel up the good times and re-jig them to suit our purposes when travelling in the modern world.

Still, there's a lot of fun to be gleaned from the things we do today, and there are still weird pastimes that live on for the would-be voyager. Soon I'll take you on to planes, trains and ships. But first, what about the pursuits which we've all (or nearly all) tried just once and found not to our liking? How can people be so keen on them?

Chapter 2

Motor bikes - and all that stuff

The younger reader will not remember, but there was a time when it was not compulsory to wear a crash helmet when riding a motorcycle or motor scooter. In those dim and distant days the freedom to wear what you like gave vent to many and varied outfits for both rider and passenger.

Because a motor bike was basically just a step up (albeit a large one) from a bicycle, the newly converted rider would hardly bother to add or subtract from the gear he or she had always worn. So it was that many a man would be seen astride a Norton or a BSA Bantam with either bicycle clips on his trouser bottoms, or even worse, with his trousers tucked haphazardly into his socks. Add to this the totally unsuitable footwear, crepe-soled shoes, 'winkle-picker' pointed toes and, yes, even galoshes and the motorised biker generally looked ridiculous from the waist down. But from the waist up he looked even worse! Following a spate of American movies about Hell's Angels and 'motorsickle' guys and gals, steaming down the freeways of California on blazing hot days, it became essential that their British equivalent also had to sport an open-necked shirt, or worse, just a T-shirt (or – in a lot of cases a string vest!) even in the chilliest of Winter weather.

Add to this the lack of driving gloves, and hence the serious rash of chilblains and the use of army surplus (both ours and Germany's!) flying goggles which were never meant for the great outdoors and consequently leaked air into the eyeballs at a steady 50 – 60 mph causing cascades of tears and 'motorbikers' squint' and you had almost the perfect example of how not to leave home.

I say 'almost' advisedly because the underdressed biker was a sight to behold, but was always outdone in the nerd stakes by the overdressed equivalent. Here is where Matty Braden came into his own. Matty who, if you were young enough, and listened long enough without nodding off, would convince you how he won the Second World War, albeit with a little help from Montgomery, Churchill and Eisenhower. Matty whom, my Dad said, fought fiercely in 1940. 'Fought?' he'd say, 'Matty fought them all the way down Spenser Street! It took four military policemen to get him in the jeep and two more to stop him sobbing!'

It appears that Private Braden spent his years of service just a little behind the battle lines. Almost twenty miles to be exact! But he did his part. Not a gunner, not a sniper – no, far more important – 'a spud barber' my Dad would recall. 'Never left an eye in a potato. A master of his craft!'

Matthew Braden was one of the forerunners of modern day motorcycle wear. His basic principle was 'better too much than too little!' As a consequence, when he appeared from 41 Spenser Street to mount his charger ('Only 125 cc but built for speed,' he would affirm) he looked as if he was wearing every stitch of clothing he owned plus maybe a few of his brother's. It was hard to say exactly what was underneath the outer shell but it made him look 3 stones heavier and was topped off by a huge army greatcoat with a hole in the centre of the back ('coward - shot in the back running away' we kids used to chuckle). Shoved into the neck area was a 20 ft long (or thereabouts) scarf which wound around and made him look like one of those African ladies with the metal rings around their hugely long necks. Each stripe of the blue and white scarf had the name of a different Everton footballer. Judging by the length, he had players who'd long since stopped running on the turf and were now pushing it up.

Over the two or three pairs of trousers he wore there was a pair of yellow oilskins which would be more at home on the North Sea waves. The lower regions were completed by a pair of Wellington boots, turned down as in the manner of the beaters in a pheasant shoot and covering at least two pairs of socks – thick wool and probably army issue.

The headwear was one of those Sherlock Holmes hats with the flaps over the ears and tightly fastened under the chin – or at least under some layers of the scarf. Add a pair of goggles with yellow glass in them which made him look like a Japanese sniper and then round it all off with a pair of gauntlets – the type and size used by a falconer and there you have Supermatt – the legend of the biking world who, with a little help, can stand up straightish and move around almost unassisted. 'But,' as he was always quick to assert, 'As warm as toast and imperious to any harm.' What a day-dreamer!

Wife Doris, the glamour of the Braden family would always dress the same, or as near as possible, and so it became impossible to work out who was who when they dismounted. On board, of course, Matty always drove and Doris hung on grimly to his waist and tried to 'relax and go with the motion of the bike' as hubby would order. Greater love hath no woman! It was an ideal combination. Ugly and overweight to look at, unsteady in full flow, unsure of its ability to stop in any given circumstance but loving and forgiving of each other's faults.

So it would have been until Eternity were it not for that curse of all classes – arthritis. As it seems to do, it hit the lady first and hardest and left 'Matt and Dot' with a major problem.

When Dot couldn't hang on to Matt's waist it became impossible for them to travel as a pair. 'Doris suffers so much,' said Matt 'that it wouldn't be fair to carry on. I couldn't be that selfish.' An admirable sentiment and one much appreciated by the bar flies in the Jaw Bone pub tap room.

'A walking saint!' is how Tucker Thompson described the modest Mr Braden.

'A man any mother would be proud of!' added Lucy Dalzell. Mind you, she said that all the time.

Yes, if Matt had only stuck to his first principles he could have gone to meet his maker leaving a legend behind. Sadly, as always in real life, he had an idea.

Having listened to odd conversations whilst at work in the chicken factory, (No, they didn't grow them – they just processed them!) and having seen the odd motorcycle scramble event on TV, Matt decided to 'bite the bullet and allow Doris back on board.' This time, though, at his side in a sidecar.

You don't see many of them now, do you? But in the heyday of Matt Braden they were everywhere. Little bubble, sometimes open-topped, sometimes completely glassed in like an aeroplane cockpit. Some in bright, even fluorescent colours, some dark and sinister in black with more black trim. Some even, as in the Bradens' case, partially green and partially rust. The green was that horrible council house colour that seemed to be everywhere in my home town. It began to spread to the length and breadth just after a paint store was opened near Miller's Bridge.

The rusty hue was literally that. Joints and seams and nuts and bolts, all untreated, lay open to the elements. A cover? Of course Matt had a cover, but only large enough to protect the engine and his seat. On occasions poor Doris would sit in her 'egg' and be almost completely awash. She was often warned by my mother that she risked lumbago, sciatica or even arthritis of the backside, while Uncle Tom would only mutter, 'Should have coated everything in Vaseline – even her bum!' There you are – the voice of an expert! Uncle Tom, who would never set foot outside to clean or repair his push-bike; Uncle Tom who took up station on the hearth rug in front of our fire to mend punctures or even to 'wipe Vaseline on his spokes.' (There's an expression you don't hear too often today.)

Still the Braden motorcycle refused to give in to the rust and weather. It seemed immune to all ills and looked like it might run forever. And although her sidecar had no roof, Doris seemed safe and secure, if a little cold and wet.

'The secret,' remarked Matty 'of our confidence in the 'flier' (as he called it) lies in the connecting bar.'

This was a piece of galvanised steel which connected bike to sidecar. It was about two feet long and bolted at each end.

'It would,' Matty assured us, 'hold a Sherman tank to a JCB with each going in opposite directions.' Praise indeed and, apparently, well justified. That is to say until 11th May – the day of disaster. The day tragedy struck!

The weather was fine and the Bradens had been for a couple of pints and a sandwich at the Stockwell Mount pub; they were returning to base when they approached the junction of Stanley and Knowsley roads. As Matt hooked the front wheel to the right and turned the bike homeward, the connecting bar which would hold a Sherman and a JCB together sheared off. The consequence was that Doris, uncontrollable and unsteerable in her egg, just careered on down Stanley Road on one wheel! A memorable sight, I'm told, as momentum overcame gravity. She would have possibly carried on to Sandhills had she not got caught in an old tram line. This jiggled her wheel to starboard and caused Doris, egg and all, to hit and break the window of Flaherty's Butchers.... Sheer speed carried her partway through the window display before she came to rest, tilted sideways, covered in tripe, black puddings and lamb chops. Other than shock and anger she appeared no worse for her trip. But then it was she vowed, 'Never again!'And she remained true to her word, rejecting all offers of a safer connecting bar, a brand new bike, and a host of proposed holiday destinations.

'What's the good of going to Eastbourne when he can't even get me home from Stanley Road?' she reasoned. And who could argue?

So - a lesson learned by us all! If you're going to

travel, always do right things and be sure of your mode of transport. Brook no imitations and insist only on the 'real thing'. Trust no-one, not even relatives by blood line or marriage; let your head rule your heart and never be over-awed by apparent technological brilliance. Remember, it's better to have never heard of a Sherman tank or a JCB than to end up in the front window of Flaherty's Butchers in Stanley Road.

Chapter 3

Buses and trams - no jams

So – if motorbike and sidecar are out of the question, where does that leave the would-be budget-minded traveller who lusts for new places and scenery?Well, obviously, in later chapters we'll be getting into rail, sea and air travel but right now I thought we'd mop up a few other worthy alternatives. Great ideas for some but, like Doris Braden knows, not for all.

I was never into walking far as a child. The length of Spenser Street was often enough for me, although when playing games I'd often run two or three times that distance. Long journeys by foot, like to school and back, were never walked for long. Chatting to school pals like Johnny Mitchell and John Rourke, would be interspersed with a little jog (ten yards or so), a walk backwards, or even sideways; a couple of leaps in the air as if heading a football, the odd skip – although this gradually disappeared as we matured past seven years old – and also long jump leaps as we tried not to step on a crack or line in the pavement. All this sufficed for day to day travel to regular places but we'd never dream of a collective route march, jog, skip, leap to anywhere new or distant.

That was left to bus or train journeys and, occasionally, a tram jaunt. For those who have never experienced a tram trip there was a special wonder in store if you were of a certain age – five to fifteen would do. You see, the trams ran on lines and were totally reversible. When one reached the terminus, instead of having to turn around, the driver would just move to the other end and take over the other set of controls. However, the great moment came when the seats had to be reversed. The backs could be altered by slamming them in the opposite direction. How we kids would sit eagerly at the terminus waiting for the driver to say, 'Can anyone give us a hand here?' and bosh! We'd be off up the aisle slamming seats for all we were worth. Often we hardly gave the people a chance to vacate them.

Both bus and tram were places of great amusement to us and we looked upon the crews as heroes, particularly the conductors. They were the men, or women (clippies) who ruled the vehicle with a rod of iron. They had leather belts like the cowboys but instead of a gun holster they supported a bag of money and the awesome ticket machine. With one clockwise turn of its little handle there would be a squawking sound and out would shoot three and a half inches of paper, suitably imprinted. Then, as a coup de grace, the conductor would rip it off with a flick of the wrist, hand it over and proceed along the aisle shouting, 'Any more fares, please?'

He or she controlled all movement by use of 'the bell'. How we longed to shout, 'When you're right, hold tight!' and then press it to prompt the driver. How we marvelled at the lines of repartee that our hero would use. For instance, when upstairs was empty and downstairs was full-ish, he would greet the passengers at the next stop with, 'Over 60's inside - all the youngsters upstairs!' It's amazing how vanity overcame lumbago in the scramble for the staircase.

Legion are the tales of catching buses and trams, running after them, just missing them and even worse! We have all suffered the late night drunken nutcase who insists on singing, swearing or attempting to throw up whilst sitting so near to us that we can smell his sweat and tobacco and alcohol-stained breath. We've all had the pseudo conman, or woman, who tries to scrounge all or part of their fare from the rest of the passengers. I'm sure, like me, you've witnessed so many odd happenings that you are now prepared to believe almost anything. I like the story (told in my hearing about a Scottish family but maybe not true) of the conductor who said to the child,

'How old are you, little boy?'

'Five' was the reply.

'And when will you be six?'

'When I get off the bus!' Who knows the truth of that?

Certainly I've made great play of my Liverpool connections when telling of the senior citizens of that great city, who are referred to as 'Twirleys'. This is because they have bus passes which are not valid until 9.00am. But the old folk stand at the stop at ten to nine saying, 'Am I too early? (Twirley)'

All these, and other apocryphal tales leave the listener in no man's land as far as the real truth but, just once in a while, there comes a gem. To fully explain the event I must take you, dear reader, back many a moon; and for those who are too young I must rake up a little of the dim and distant past.

Before pop groups, beat groups and punk or heavy metal bands, music was of a more sedate nature. We sang folky type tunes or country and western – or my particular favourite, skiffle! Skiffle was a kind of mixture of everything but essentially played and sung in the most basic way. No synthesisers, no brass and reed ensembles, no string sections. No, a more simple approach was needed. A washboard, used to launder clothes and with a glass or metal face, would be stroked vigorously by fingers covered in needlework thimbles. This produced the snare drum effect ideal for backing songs about railroads.The melody would be produced by blowing (or doo-de-dooing) into a kazoo – a weird and wonderful creation. God knows what sort of brain came up wtih that. An old Spanish or folk guitar (unelectrified!) produced the chords to back the kazoo - and the bass .... well, the bass was something else and is the nub of my story. (True honestly!)

For those too young to recall, the skiffle group bass instrument comprised a tea chest, some twine and a broom handle. The twine connected the upturned chest to one end of the handle and the other end was then placed on the chest top. By plucking at the twine a lowish note could be produced and this could be varied by levering the handle back and forth. Musically it left a lot to be desired but who cared? The major problem for the bass player was transport. It was easy for the washboard man to carry his instrument under his arm, or under his duffle coat if he chose anonymity. The guitarist had a canvas type case to sling over his shoulder and the kazoo player usedhis top pocket. But the tea chest was a different thing altogether.

Generally, a second band member or even a camp follower would help. 'Just give us a touch with this to the bus stop, will you?' was an oft-heard plea on a Saturday night after a gig. The lifting and shifting done, the next problem was getting the thing on a bus or tram. Generally, conductors were sympathetic and would allow the 'instrument' to be placed in the space on the platform where people got on. There it would stand, chest rightway up with handle placed inside and sticking up. Other than a little lateral movement the whole affair remained free from the threat of slipping off. Never a problem in the world except for one Saturday night and one drunken docker trying to catch the last bus home from the Pier Head in Liverpool. Having staggered drunkenly but happily from a distant wine lodge, our hero found himself still twenty yards from the tail of the Corporation bus which was leaving the stop. Breaking into a mixture of jog, shuffle and mini heart attack he gradually started to overtake his prey. Glancing up in the half light and through a wine-ish haze he saw the platform of the bus and what appeared to be the pole people grabbed to assist when boarding. Reaching out at full stretch he grasped it in his fingers and, in trying to lever himself aboard, realised it was the handle of the bass. His momentum yanked it towards him and off the bus came handle, twine and tea chest – the latter ending up on top of him, leaving him lying in the road looking like a tortoise with a cube shaped shell with a head and limbs sticking out.

When I first heard that story I laughed at how ridiculous it sounded. Later I was never quite sure.

We've all got a lot to thank the bus service for, not least the provision of shelters to harbour a woebegotten soul after a late night on the town. It also gave us security and a feeling of freedom of movement, albeit slightly reined in by time limits. Where would the young swains of yesteryear be without the last bus home, or the first of the morning – the forerunner of the 'red eye'. Probably more apt would be the title 'bleary eye and yellow of pallor'.

It seems incredible today to think that a young man's entire Saturday night could be spent in a dance hall or disco, not dancing but working out who would be the most attractive or least unattractive girl to escort home whilst keeping inside the time scale and range of the local bus timetable. Many must have been the lasses who lived too far away to tempt the young romeos. Who did they ever settle down with? How, in fact, did they ever get home? Of course there was a code of chivalry between the blokes and information was passed as if by jungle drum.

'Where are you from love?'

'Manchester, me and me mate.'

'Well thanks for the dance - see you!'

Back at the bar, 'Anyone from Manchester? Two of yours over there!'

Of course, those days have almost faded totally from memory. Today there are far more ways of to-ing and fro-ing to the big city. But the lure of public transport is still there. Still holding a prime position in our lives. How would the major cities and towns survive if every visitor came by car - and generally only one or two to a vehicle?

So the buses and, still in some cities I'm happy to say, trams, continue to brighten our lives. May they long provide their excellent service. Today, when lots of them are one person operated we still cling on to the legend of the conductor with the lightning fast repartee.

'Do you stop at the Dorchester Hotel?'

'What – on my wages?'

May that sort of tale continue despite the onrush of scientific progress, like the trainee one man bus driver whose vehicle careered off the road and into a hedge.

'What happened, Driver?' asked a newly arrived police officer.

'I don't know' was the reply, 'I was upstairs collecting fares at the time!'

So, keep your mind firmly set on the fun of bus and tram travel. Be mindful of the range of services both in distance and time scale. Remember fare charges and always try to have 'the right money' on your person. Don't be the twit with the £50 note who's only going two stops. And, no matter what the cost, it probably still is the cheapest and safest way to travel.

Chapter 4

Bikes, John Kenny and Dockers

Before I launch into long distance travel and the benefits and fun associated with trains and boats and planes let me mop up the other forms of transport which we have, in our short time on Earth, experienced. Who recalls scooters - no, not motorised, but the early form of what has recently become a modern day craze? It seems weird now to the older, more jaundiced eye, to have kids free-wheeling and push scooting along the pavements and streets of our nation. Did we find it so much fun? Would we like to do it again if we dared? Of course we did – and would! What a great feeling of freedom and sense of self-sufficiency that weird object gave us. What miles we pounded in all weathers totally free of punctures, petrol gauges, dangerous toxic fumes and death or injury from excessive speeds.

Speed yes - just how fast did we go? Certainly more than walking pace, so maybe five or six miles per hour. Multiply that by the four or so hours that we were outdoors and that is some distance my friend. In a straight line, and not returning home, it's amazing just how far we could have gone.A little like the woman who was becoming sick of her husband's constant grumbling and hypochondria, who asked her GP for advice:-

'He should walk seven miles every day,' stated the medic.'

Will that cure him?' asked the lady eagerly.

'No,' said the doctor 'But in a week he'll be forty-nine miles away from you!'

But seriously. Scooters were great fun for us youngsters, but they did have one great drawback, nay pitfall. Before I go into it I want all mothers to cast their minds back to when their own offspring used this mode of transport and try to recall the biggest bugbear to their sanity. I'll give you a clue – footwear!

Yes, there without doubt is the rub. The wear and tear of the shoes we wore. The constant pounding which they received from pavement, tarmac and all else, gradually had an eroding effect. The big trouble was, though, that it generally affected only one shoe. How often, oblivious to the consequences, did we slam down our stronger foot to propel the 'machine' and leave the other safely and wear-free on the scooter.

This meant that, unless a child became two-footed in the scooting action, the toll on footwear became twice as excessive as it should be. It also led to a million mothers attempting to buy odd shoes to make up the shortfall. I'm surprised some enterprising shoe-makers and retailers didn't come up with 'three pack' offers featuring two shoes of the stronger foot.

This would have also helped replace the damaged soles and heels of the lesser roller skate wearers. I say 'lesser' because it wasn't, nor isn't, every child who could manage to stay upright and steady on a pair of roller skates. Certainly in our street there were many who preferred to use only one and to scoot along by pushing with the other foot. This had two advantages over the fully shod roller skates. First it was almost free of accidents and breakages.

'Look Mum – no hands!' CRASH!! 'Look Mum – no teeth!'

Second, because the early skates were not specific as to which feet they belonged, twice as many kids could partake of the fun at no extra cost.

This surely was the primitive ancestor of skateboards as we know them today, although just how far we'd have got with all the acrobatics that are now performed the Lord only knows.

Still, some sort of wheels attached to the feet, either by straps or gravity are certainly a major help when travelling. Ask any waiter in the major cities who has to cover acres of pavement delivering drinks or meals. As long as there's a clear run then the principle is ideal.

But of course, when I say wheels beneath the feet, I must always include bicycles as one of the ideal modes of transport known to man or woman kind. From those halcyon days of the penny-farthing – one big wheel, one little wheel – to the mountain bikes, rally bikes and racing bikes of today, there has always been an attraction to the metal beasts that require no foot, no fuel and only a little 'Vaseline on the spokes' to quote Uncle Tom.

From the baby days of trying to be big enough to sit on a tricycle without slipping off, we've all dreamed of that magic day when a two wheeled steed was presented to us. 'Just have a go and see what you think.' They had to be the sweetest words to a youngster's ears.

Do you, like me, remember the first basic instructions? 'Look straight ahead and not at the front wheel!' A simple enough thing to say but not as easy to do. It's a bit like crossing a ravine with the encouragement of a friend saying,

'It's a five hundred feet drop but don't look down.'

There never seemed to be an easy way to go from still to cycling on a bike. Mini stabilising wheels may have given the impression of free biking but really they still left a void between aided and unaided. We probably all began with a balancing act from a friend or relative holding us upright and giving a reassuring push. It's hard, even now, to explain the feeling of elation when realising they had let go and you were on your own. 'Today Spenser Street,' I remember thinking, 'Tomorrow the world!' (Or at least Marsh Lane).

Of course, riding and manoeuvring the vehicle was only the beginning. Lots of new information had to be gleaned and memorised. How to fix a puncture, how to alter seat and handlebar settings, how to oil gear chains, how to 'Vaseline your spokes.' And, of course, the prime lesson – which bicycle clips to buy. Tucking trouser legs into socks was a definite no-no. Even today there is no dafter sight than a man, woman or child dismounting a cycle, or motorcycle, looking like they're wearing a cheap version of plus fours. No, no! Dignity must always prevail.

I suppose it was an early sign of chauvinism but I always felt glad I was a boy because I could own a bike with a crossbar. This enabled me to give a lift to a pal, and even make it a threesome with another straddling the metal plate behind my seat which was really a support for a saddle bag. Yes, it was a 'boy thing' that gave us the impression that we resembled the cowboy heroes of our youth. The horse became the bike and all possible needs and wants could be transported aboard her – no matter how far or how arduous the journey ahead should be.

Perhaps you began your cycling career astride a bone-shaker of a second hand machine which would leave lots of refinements to be desired. You know, simple things like mudguards, a pump, lights and, quite often, brakes. The latter were all right if you had them and they were in good nick. But I always found replacing brake blocks a tedious duty and oft neglected to do so. How envious I was of the child whose bike had a fixed wheel'. You know the type. They turned at all times and there was no way to free wheel. This, at least, gave a secondary form of stopping – albeit at the expense of maximum leg effort which entailed virtually standing upright whilst still keeping the feet on the pedals. Of course the drawback to the fixed wheel was the fact that the rider couldn't free wheel down hill and so had to pedal at all times. The one, some thought illegal, bonus of having this type of steed was the ability to travel at really low speeds whilst keeping control. 'Boko' McCann, a school pal of mine – so called because he couldn't pronounce the French word 'beaucoup' properly, was the seven consecutive year winner of the slow bike race at our school sports day. Although extremely tall and gangly he could almost freeze aboard his mount and just stay there whilst all around him wobbled and wibbled. Some cynics suggested that a lot of his lack of momentum was down to the fact that the 'whole thing was rusted together anyway.' Jealousy, jealousy!

But enough of the fixed wheel and back to the road -

or at least the preparations and planning we went through before we ventured forth.

On any sort of run longer than once around the block there had to be serious discussion. Would the journey start and finish in daylight? If not then provision had to be made about lights. Generally speaking this was easily dealt with. Between the group, sometimes numbered ten or twelve, we'd continue to borrow or save up to buy, one front and one rear light. Thus the column leader and the trail man would be showing the necessary white and red whilst the other ten or so middle men would strive to keep in line and as close as possible to the person directly in front. You think today's juggernauts and trailers are long vehicles? You should have seen the faces of the motorists who overtook us, particularly if the red light was at one end of a bend and the white was sixty yards further on around the corner!

So – with the illumination situation solved there was soon no end to the distance we could travel – given the necessary safeguards - and weather protection. Indeed one of the major threats to any British activity is rain. Rain predicted, rain unpredicted, rain that sneaks up on you even out of a clear blue sky. To counter the rain was the biker's coverall which consisted of a huge sheet of yellow plastic which went over the head and shoulders like Pancho Villa's poncho and then was neatly arranged over the saddle at the back and the handlebars at the front. This garment, allied with a sou'wester hat kept the wearer almost bone dry if a little ridiculous to look at. So the rider was free from the threat of God's wrath and the machine was rust-proofed with Vaseline, but what about the weakest link – the tyres?

The dreaded puncture was always a hovering sword of Damacles to we young knights of the road. It could, like rain, happen at any time and bring chaos to a day out. The answer was, of course, a puncture repair kit and a set of inner-tube valves. Generally speaking one kit could cater for the needs of several riders and so the onus was usually placed on the leader of the pack or the 'boss of our gang' as we called him.

He, or in Emily Green's case, she had the sole responsibility for puncture repairs and valve replacements and also had to have tyre levers to ease the tyre off and on the wheel rim. This and one or two other items would be kept on the leader's back in a haversack, ensuring that precautions were not only carried out, but were seen to be carried out.

So the physical side of the bicycle and all its parts were deemed to be catered for and at least doubly so when one or even more of the group procured a bell for the handlebars. It left time for just a cursory look at the physical side of the cyclists.

Obviously speed and distance had to be regulated to cover the broad range of ability and endurance which the group encompassed. Also allowance must be made for the discomfort of girls in skirts riding bikes with crossbars; modesty must always prevail over reckless speed and wind conditions.

But, looming large above these items was the logistical spectre of catering for the massed group. With only saddle bags, and not too many of them, or haversacks, which not too many girls (Emily Green excepted) fancied toting; the provision of fodder for the troops became of paramount importance. Obviously there was the usual picnic fare, but that would be augmented by performance enhancing items like bottles of Lucozade (aids recovery), Mars bars (for work, rest and play) and a myriad of other titbits that we'd seen advertised and recommended. (Would you believe even the most basic of human needs – a bread and dripping sandwich?)

Occasionally the brighter gang members would bring medicines (Aspros) and balms (calamine lotion) and other aids to health and survival, like a jar of Vaseline for sunburn, scrapes, bruises- and spokes. All of this helped to promote a feeling of confidence and high spirits amongst the troops. Very little thought was given to money. We thought more of 'living off the land'.

Our destinations would vary depending on our day to day requirements. One fun jaunt would be a run of about six miles to a local lane called Chestnut Avenue where one could find 'millions of conkers'.

'A boy in our class filled three sacks with them last week!'

'Oh, really? And where did they fit on his bike?'

Another venue would be the beach (or pale shadow thereof) that stretched Northwards from Liverpool's Gladstone Dock. Mucky sand, shingle, very little sun but loads of fun!

Of course, more serious matters could also dictate our route and distance - haircuts for instance. Can you remember as a young boy or girl going to have a haircut and being accompanied by mum who insisted she knew more about your locks than you did yourself?

'More off around the ears.'

'Shorter at the back.'

'His father will go mad if you leave it like that.' So my Mother would bray on until an exasperated barber would snap, 'Look love, make your mind up. I can cut it off but if it all goes wrong I can't stick it back on again!'

During this duel of wits the one person the cutter hardly looked at was the poor waif sitting in the chair –

or on a plank placed across the chair. So the 'final cut' would often look appalling with bits sticking out and chunks missing. The whole sin of follicle destruction would then be covered by the application of some thick greasy goo which stuck everything down and was the forerunner of super glue. Yes, most hairdressers, under orders, would destroy or at least wreak havoc with a child's head covering. But not Dirty Jack!

Dirty Jack was the children's man. Dirty Jack was our shelter in troubled times. In a cruel world it's good to have someone to rely upon and the man from Fazakerley was such a person. He it was who gave our hair style, who took his time clipping the back, sides and fringe with the same care and technique – not a raving mad charge at all parts with the clippers. His was more art than attack and we would crawl over broken glass to put our heads in his hands. Actually, the journey to Fazakerley was almost the same sort of ordeal. A round trip of some fourteen miles over all kinds of dodgy terrain, cobbles, tarmac and dirt tracks and, the greatest threat to the junior cyclist – tram lines!

Sorry was the tale often told about the boy from Litherland who sadly took his eye off the road for a split second and ended up with his front wheel wedged in the metal groove of the tram line. This was followed rapidly by the back wheel and neither would come free no matter how hard he tried. The whole affair concluded with the victim having to pedal himself down to the tram sheds, at one point being pursued hotly by a Number 17! Only sterling work by a ticket inspector managed to dislodge the bike and save the lad from a lifetime raiding the rails.

Luckily, no such fate ever came our way and the trips to Dirty Jack's were always a pleasure if a little long and tiring. Sometimes the seven miles back in the wind and rain gave us a chance to shake free the bits of hair so carefully snipped and still lodged in our ears and on our necks.

Over the years we gradually went less and less to Jack's and soon stopped altogether. And yet, in all the years of trusting him with our locks we never found out why his nickname was Dirty Jack. He seemed well dressed and groomed and never used abusive language. He appeared a paragon of virtue – so why 'dirty'?

It was only a year or so ago I found the answer from a distant relative. His second name was Pye – the same as the very famous wrestler who thrilled audiences in the forties, fifties and sixties with his exploits and foul deeds, always apparently vicious but really totally harmless. So 'Dirty Jack Pye' of the ring had inadvertently bestowed the title upon a likeable, lovable snipper who was the children's hero.

As the demands of the great big outside world began to rain down on our ever-maturing beings we sought perfection in all things, particularly in our recreation. So it was that the simple boneshaker, bought for a quid, bikes were slowly abandoned in favour of more sleek machines. Overnight we discovered gears that allowed us to alter the pedal speed for differing conditions. First it was the Sturmey Archer type three-gear, simple to click into system or its like. Slowly that developed into the huge eight or ten gear set-ups which seemed to drown the features of the back wheel in chain, and deliver more and more complicated levers and pulleys for us to adapt to.

The old standard bell was replaced by the time trial type – the 'one ding variety' as my Uncle Tom called it. And along with these came the sleek new wheels – narrow of gauge, lighter by design and use of alloys larger in diameter and another help in our quest for speed and comfort. Of course new doesn't always mean comfortable. Take the seat for instance. In the old days the standard bicycle seat was like an armchair – highly sprung and designed to envelop the bottom. But as other innovations became more streamlined so did the seat, or 'saddle' as we now called it. Torture Chamber would have been a better title because of the effect that the tiny rock hard leather hump had on our nether regions.

Add the solid unsprung rear end to the craze for 'drop handlebars' that lowered the entire body frame at the front, and left the rear end higher than the head, and you've got the ideal cycling position for a deformed person. Still it wasn't all gloom. Along came drinks holders, complete with straw, to fasten to the handlebars for easy quaffing of the latest energy-enhancing drinks. Pedal clips were added to make sure the feet stayed in place. There was even a slick and easy-to-operate dynamo system for front and rear lights - to be followed years later by mountain bikes and the latest in microlite racing bikes, the metal mounts of our adolescence were a thing of wonder if not joy.

'Each to his own,' as they say, and the latest improvements eventually allowed all of God's creatures to find the perfect solution to their travel needs. There wasn't a need that couldn't be satisfied, from the simplest to the most obscure. Take John Kenny!

John Kenny was what we'd call, today, an 'anorak' – an avid fan of things most obscure – a person who dedicated hours, days and yes even years of his life to the increase in personal knowledge of topics others thought mundane. He was the one out of step when it came to gang decisions; he was the one who knew too much for the rest of us but had no way of forcing home his point of view. Why, he even knew virtually the whole list of popes in history, including the legendary 'Sixtus the Fifth'. But it wasn't knowledge or learning that made John Kenny a legend – it was speed.

At no time during our early days did we cyclists attempt to compete in speed trials or endurance runs. Due consideration was given to the shortcomings of others' equipment and physical stature and no stress was ever put on the meek and weak to try to equal the strong. But those rules only applied to the human aspect of speed and ability. What about man against the elements?

Sure, we'd all stretched our collective capabilities to the limit in distance covered per hour and per day but now the most dangerous unknowns entered the equation – time and speed.

There had been legendary stories of children from other gangs reaching ten or even fifteen miles per hour in level or at least only slightly inclined runs, although no genuine proof had been, nor could be, revealed. But to the mind of a sturdier ruminator and fanatic, these stories were a red rag to a bull. How to outdo the unknown speedsters? How to not only travel faster but be seen to travel faster? How to live on record for ever? John Kenny had the answer. The bus! Yes, the great big double-decker, Corporation green or Ribble red bus. What a pacemaker! What a wind breaker! What a great and accurate way of measuring speed over a set stretch of good road! Follow the bus! So simple that it was unbelievable that no-one else had ever thought of it. John had seen news footage in the cinema of World cycle records being assisted by cars trailing huge wooden baffle boards being followed tightly by a madly pedalling athlete. To his agile and sometimes over-fertile mind this set up was nothing compared with the massive shield provided by local bus, added to which there was no expense, no definite time restrictions (they ran every few minutes) and all the world, or a least most of Bootle, could see for themselves his efforts and success.

In a nutshell, the plan was to measure the distance between various stops Using a speedometer/distance checker that only an anorak would know of. This connected to the front wheel of the bike and was remarkably accurate. Next it was important to time a bus from stop to stop and, working backwards, work out its average speed. Then, with a couple of minor adjustments it should be possible to work out the bus's maximum speed from stop to stop. Having done all this, and gaugeing that at its fastest the bus could be travelling at about 25 mph, it was only necessary to get behind it at one stop and pedal like mad as closely to it as possible for as long as possible, or at least until it slowed down.

In an ideal world this would have resulted in a new land speed record, at least for north Bootle, and a laurel wreath for John Kenny. Poor John Kenny! A man before his time possibly. Certainly a man before brake lights on buses. A simple standard fitting today but in our youth a thing never heard or dreamed of. Too bad! How sad – particularly for a would-be record holder pedalling like a mad thing on half cobbles, half tarmac, oblivious of all around him, head bent and body arched (as dropped handlebars demanded) following a bus which suddenly had to jam its brakes on to avoid hitting Ernie Reynolds. Ernie was a seafarer, merchant navy type who had worked for Cunard for twenty-five years. 'Been round the World two dozen times and never dropped a plate,' he would boast.

Ernie made a habit, when on shore leave to go to the local music store and buy the entire top twenty discs and spend his entire days and most of his nights playing them at about 2000 decibels and quaffing beer and whisky whilst stamping his right foot to the rhythm. 'One leg Logan' my Dad named him. 'The man who never sleeps' was my Mother's description.

On the fateful day of the record bid, Ernie had been in the pub for three hours treating all and sundry to drinks and getting well plastered. 'I knew he was drunk' attested the landlord 'because people were talking rubbish and Ernie could understand them!'

Staggering into the street and ignoring his kerb drill, our naval hero decided to proceed directly across Stanley Road to the music shop shrugging off yells of warning and motor horns. It's even probable that he failed to hear the screech of the bus' tyres as the driver strained every sinew to miss him.

'Stopped the bus on a penny' enthused an onlooker. 'Brilliant driving. Totally avoided a collision.'

Well, at least a collision at the front end! At the rear it was a different story. John Kenny, as oblivious as Ernie Reynolds to the brake noise, had no idea that anything was amiss until he actually hit the bus. From as close as he was it was a little more than a collision; it was more of a catapult launching - nice to watch on aircraft carriers but previously unknown on Stanley Road. In a way it was good that the bus had a platform because it meant that John's head didn't strike anything for about twenty feet.

Apparently he just glided past a dozen or so pairs of incredulous eyes and headed driverward, giving a whole new meaning to the order, 'Move along the bus please!' Had it not been for the stout lady who'd been shopping for the new latex pillows and had placed them in front of her legs behind the driver's cabin, who knows what might have befallen young Kenny. As it was he suffered concussion, bruising, cuts, abrasions and damaged pride. Ernie Reynolds suffered naught as he reeled across to the record store oblivious of damage, confusion and loss of cycling world record.

A sad tale to tell, of course, but a definite exception to the general rule that cycling is both a safe and convenient means of travel. How much more convenient to park a bike than a car! How much easier to negotiate traffic jams and snarl-ups! How much healthier to use with regard to exercise and all round fitness. But with all its benefits the bicycle can still give rise to problems.

Take 'the Home Secretary'. He was one of the elite band of Liverpool men known as dockers. Each was a hard-working son of toil and each was admired by the youngsters as the last of the gunfighters. Dockers were the backbone of mine and many another town. Men who worked hard, sometimes in atrocious conditions to keep open the sealanes of Great Britain. Every man was a one-off. There were no carbon copies and to prove it each one had a nickname.

'The bald cat' who was heard to say on a bus, 'I've lost me fare!'

'The sick pigeon' who never left the loft.

'The destroyer' - always looking for a sub.

'The wonder boy' – 'I wonder what's in this crate?

'Even the dock gate policeman called 'The Balloon ' who used to plead, 'Don't let me down fellers!' My own personal favourites were men I actually met whilst working on the docks during holidays from college.

'Harry the Horse' apparently derived his name from a Damon Runyon novel and he was known by nothing else. I well recall the classic day when Harry was missing from the gang. The boss arrived and asked the bloke next to me, 'Where's Harry the Horse?' to which my comrade replied, 'I haven't seen head nor tail of him all day!' Still a legendary line!

But wait, I stray away from the 'Home Secretary' – Jack Regan. His title was a simple expression of the everyday facts of dockers' lives. Jack lived nearby and at any given excuse - tea-break, lunch-break or whatever - he would simply 'go home'. Naturally, considering the distance to be travelled he needed pedal power and so it became imperative that he exactly positioned his bike when parking to gain maximum time for the homeward dash.

Often he would spend twenty minutes or more deciding where the gang would have reached in shifting cargo so that he could simply hop aboard and disappear in a cloud of dust, or in our case – flour!

'You're a mathematician,' he said to me. 'You should be able to work out the exact place to leave my bike.'

Much as I tried I never quite got it to the exact spot because, as we moved along the quay loading sacks on to trucks we would often be hampered by ropes snapping or sacks bursting. Jokingly, I once suggested he brought two bikes – one to ride home and the other for us to re-position for him as we moved along. He almost swallowed it.

Probably the greatest day in docks history was when the Home Secretary came to work on a tandem. He was accompanied by the Spaceman (he used to go to Ma's for lunch) and they made a stately, if somewhat ugly to look at, entrance through the gates of the Canada Dock. Of course the bike took a lot longer to position because of its length but eventually the pair were happy.

Tea-break came and went and so did they. So too with lunch break. But at the end of the day the Secretary broke all rules by going, not straight home, but to the local pub, accompanied by the Spaceman riding shotgun. After much drinking and hilarity the dynamic duo boarded their long wheel base steed and set off in the general direction of Seaforth Sands, pedalling gently and trusting to luck. However, at the first set of traffic lights tragedy struck. They both braked at the sign of the red signal but neither remembered to put their foot on the floor for balance. And so, slowly and gracefully, the whole kit and caboodle leaned and then, ever so slowly, fell to the tarmac - a sight still talked about today in the alehouses of Merseyside!

Such a happening today would probably not incur the injuries our two heroes suffered (scrapes, bruises, lumps on foreheads) because of the modern day protective clothing – helmet, padding, gloves, cycle pants, specially developed shoes and so on. And essential as these have become, there are still hazards to the comfort and safety of the rider.

Punctures are still the bane of the cyclist's life and no sensible person would leave home without a repair kit in the saddle bag. Theft, of course, was and still is prevalent on the bicycle front. Even forty or fifty years ago it was almost compulsory to carry a lock and chain to attach the bike to a lamp-post or other immoveable object. Sometimes however thieves would zero in on the more exclusive machines with bolt cutters or hacksaws. So security became paramount. I remember in the fifties and sixties cycling to football matches and paying sixpence to park my bike in the backyard of a house near the ground. I wonder if they still do that today?

Of course, today's exclusive machines are a far cry from the old sit up and beg, or drop handlebar jobs of yesteryear. Now with the advent of lightweight materials, and computerised streamlining the better bikes have risen to the thousand pounds plus range – much dearer than my first mount – £5, or my first brand new one - £17! But such is progress! And such is the attitude to cycling and values today. It is best explained by examining the mind of a child.

Although a thousand pounds plus is a lot of money, and undoubtedly it buys more elegant and state of the art machinery, I wonder sometimes if the overall effect on the young cyclist who receives it as a gift is comparable with the little 'do-it-yourself' modifications that transformed yesterday's bikes. I can remember the feeling of elation when shown how to affix a folded piece of cardboard, or a strip of plastic to the mudguard (there's a word you don't hear much nowadays!) and into the spokes of the rear wheel. On the wheel turning the card or plastic flapped with every spoke and gave the sound of a full-size motorbike – well, at least a smallish one!

Another big attraction was the delivery bike with the huge well in the front which held a basket. Built to carry the butcher's, or baker's, orders of meat, bread and so on these giants of the highway generally carried more children in the basket than goods. Many a time I've sat in one with my legs dangling over the front, oblivious to any danger or threat of rain, snow or act of God. It's amazing how that wonder of the delivery service has been compacted into a sleek machine with panniers and saddlebags which today deliver pizzas and takeaways to your door. Isn't it also strange that because of the use of these bicycles and the street knowledge of their riders it is quicker to get a meal to your door than an ambulance!

So, many years on from its first appearance on the roads of the world, the humble bicycle continues to develop and continues to play a major part in our lives. Where would the young generation be today without their two-wheeled chariots? How else would we parents appreciate the eagerness and awe with which youngsters anticipate the gift of such a beast? And in the mind of a child, all things are possible – even the impossible!

I love the story of the youngster and his dad at the Christmas Grotto in the big city store. Santa had gone into his well tried and trusted routine, including a couple of, 'Ho-Ho-Hos' when he came out with the burning question, 'And what would you like for Christmas my little man?'

'A mountain bike, please,' replied he nipper. Behind the youngster's back his dad was making huge 'No!' gestures to the man in red, furiously shaking his head and wiping a finger across his Adam's apple area in a 'cut my throat' gesture.

Catching on to the meaning, and the possibility of dad not being able to afford such a luxury the grey-bearded old gent said, 'I don't think I've any mountain bikes left. I'm sorry.'

'Ah, but Santa,' murmured the little 'un. 'You must have one.'

'But even if I did find one,' said Santa, thinking quickly, 'I wouldn't be able to get it down your chimney!'

Just as father's panic started to abate, the little fellow said, 'Well – you got a snooker table down it last year!'

In one guise or another I guess bikes will be with us forever. And judging by the numbers of cars, caravans and jeeps that are on main roads going coastward each weekend laden with two, three or even more machines, families are still enjoying the pleasures that they bring.

So on you go – you twenty-first century pedallers!

May all your slopes be downwards, and may all your tyres remain inflated. Remember, any travel is fun if you obey the rules. Check directions, protection, sustenance and, most of all, reliability.

Take cover, take food, take repair kits and, of course, take care.

Chapter 5

Let the train take the strain

I suppose, when travelling under one's own steam, there is always a possibility of disaster, be it totally self-inflicted or the result of faulty repairs of lack of adequate checking procedure. How many times have we heard stories of fan belts snapping in cars, engines starved of oil or, worst of all, front wheels coming off bikes whilst the rider is in full flow. It happened to me on Peggy Rawlings' bike and, believe me, it's not funny. The memory I will always retain is the length of time - no more than a split second - that felt like a day as the bike stayed upright before the obvious front end drop that catapulted me to earth. All these, and a myriad other calamities, seem to be lurking near the surface whenever self-propulsion is involved. But not so when we are within the comfort and steady rhythmic motion of a train.

Probably it is as a result of the many movies we've seen over the years picturing the Orient Express, the humble steam trains, or the mighty diesels that we all tend to look upon rail travel as the leisurely way to go. Sure, it has a different appeal when we are traveling as fast as possible to work or to an appointment and the whole shebang is being jeopardized by late arrivals, signal failures, line works and even 'go-slows'. But, that apart, when the train is there to transport us to a holiday destination or, in the case of the Orient Express and the like, is itself the holiday, well then a completely new world becomes our oyster

Close your eyes with me and try to recall those magic moments, comic events and tragic tales with happy endings that have happened to us in our short lifetimes on earth - and on train lines.

My first recollection of rail travel was when I was about four years old and I took my first trip on the Liverpool overhead railway that ran for miles along the line of the docks and was called 'The Dockers' Umbrella'. From its windows I watched the hundreds of ships docking and loading and unloading and sailing. The colours of their funnels, their superstructures, their masts were a wonderful sight and made me dream of the fabulous voyages that they made, and that one day I too would make. How lucky I am that all these things came to pass – but then that's for another chapter.

Right now I'm thinking of the comic rather than the romantic side of rail travel and am reminded immediately of the gag about the weary looking man alighting from the Liverpool-London train at Euston Station saying, 'Well, that's the hardest part of the journey over.'

'Oh, really,' said a fellow passenger, 'and where is your final destination?'

'Karachi!' Sighed Mr Weary.

You can almost see the ending coming, can't you? It's

as if certain people have been selected by a higher being to suffer the slings, arrows and discomforts of a life on the iron horse, thankfully to the amusement and entertainment of the rest of us. And, as I'm sure you know, we've only to scratch the surface of a seasoned traveller to find the humour. The story that started my research on trains was told by my pal, Brian.

Like many of the older generation my dearest love of all was watching steam trains. Their bright livery and their gleaming mechanical parts seemed to have been continually steam-cleaned by the powerful jets of smoke that billowed from the engine: the piercing whistle that would sound, it seemed, for no particular reason at all but simply at the driver's whim. The clatter of metal running over metal as wheels met rails, as they 'clacked' and 'clicketeyed' where two separate lengths of rail met and left an ever so small gap between.

All this, and the one-off smell of the coal-burning engine and the trail of smoke which engulfed train and bystanders alike. On a Summer's day what better sight or smell or sound could there be? It appeared that nothing could disturb this little piece of man-made Heaven which ran through your town and mine, laden with happy, cheerful travellers whose lives were so idyllic that nothing could possibly shatter the magic. Nothing, that is, except my pal, Brian.

A lovely man, now retired, who pursued the tailors' and outfitters' trade, having left his National Service as an airman and personally protecting the whole of Western Europe against Communism simply by his presence. A man given to 'enlarging the truth' by differing degrees depending on his intake of gin and tonic, but a wonderful story teller, tipsy or no. So good in fact that it became almost impossible to separate fact from fantasy. As opposed to rail travel, the journeys of his mind had no gaps between the rails and so there was never a giveaway 'clickety clack' – just a chuckle and a flick of the forelock.

And so it was ordained that Brian's top train story would go down in history as very possibly, almost probably, true. If not totally true, then certainly partly true. Unlike the curate's egg – 'good in parts' - his tale was good all through. Too good to be true? You tell me!

It came to pass that Brian had been attending an exhibition of clothing in London and was returning aboard a corridor train to Birmingham. Never a heavy smoker, he enjoyed the odd cigarette, or cigarillo on special occasions, and this was one, because he'd set up a few good deals. The only compartment with any reasonable amount of room in it contained just two folks, obviously man and wife, seated opposite each other in the prime seats by the window.

Brian eased himself into a doorside seat with a cheery, 'Good afternoon,' which received neither answer nor even recognition. So, with a shrug of the shoulders he opened his paper, took out a pen for the crossword and decided that, comfortable and safe in the arms of the steam train driver and his crew, he'd celebrate with a cigarette. Big mistake! Not only were his fellow travellers too ignorant to exchange greetings, but they were manically anti-smoking. Hardly had Brian produced a packet of Senior Service than the man opened a window and the woman began to cough. What to do? Well, discretion being the better part, the fags were replaced and Brian was left twiddling his thumbs in silence.

This scenario could possibly have lasted for eternity had the train not pulled in to Banbury on a scheduled stop. Hardly had the wheels come to rest and the loud blast of hissing steam poured from the engine than The

Glums ('les miserables' Brian later named them) shot to their feet, scooped up briefcase and handbag, bundled their way unceremoniously past Brian's swiftly retracting legs and were gone.

Whew! What a relief, as if a dull thudding pain had been suddenly relieved. Probably a thudding pain would have been more welcome. Still, not to worry. The world was now all right again and it was time to relax and enjoy the window view as the train began to pull out. However, in moving seats Brian casually looked up and was stunned to see that The Glums had left a suitcase on the luggage rack

In a flat spin our hero yanked it down and, running along the corridor dragging the case in his wake, reached a door and flung it open. Luckily there was a porter on the platform and Brian screamed to him, 'They must still be on the platform! Their name is on the suitcase!'

Now, to be honest, having been treated so shabbily by the couple I'm not so sure I'd have gone to that much trouble. I'd have been more likely to let them reap what they sowed by their forgetfulness. Nonetheless, the deed was done and my friend sat back and relaxed in the knowledge that his actions had eased the burden of his fellow man, irrespective of how obnoxious that man was.

Obnoxious? Obnoxious? Believe me, friend, you don't know obnoxious; not unless you witnessed what happened next. As Brian stretched out and placed his feet on the seat opposite, and slowly inhaled on a Senior Service cigarette and exhaled smoke through the compartment, the door slid open and there appeared Mr and Mrs Glum! Apparently they had only gone to the buffet car for tea and biscuits and were back as large as life!

'Oh!' muttered the smoker from his reclined position, 'It's you.'

'And who else were you expecting?' enquired Mr Glum, coughing as he spoke and wafting away the smoke curls.'

Well, it's just that I thought you'd got off at Banbury.'

'Got off at Banbury? And what business would it have been of yours if we had?' snorted 'Mr-Glum-turned-ugly'?

'Well, it's just your suitcase, you see,' muttered a petrified Brian.'

My suitcase,' bellowed 'ugly' as he looked up and saw it gone. 'My God, my suitcase! What have you done with it?'

'Well,' squealed Brian, 'I threw I off the train.'

'Threw it off? My God, have you taken leave of your senses, man? We're going to Stranraer!'

'Look,' said my pal, 'Here's my card. If I can't get the case to you in the next day or so I'll pay for all you've lost.'

Slightly less glum, but just as annoyed, the couple eventually simmered down and retook their seats at the window. Brian hastened to the bar and swallowed five or six large brandies in an effort to still his beating heart and calm what was left of his shattered nerves.

Arriving at his own station our hero made his way very unsteadily to the porter's cabin to report the incident and hopefully recover the suitcase. You may remember that in those days porters' cabins had a wooden flap-type shutter that could be raised or lowered over the window. This flap luckily was up and behind it sat a red-faced, not altogether co-operative British Rail porter.

'Can you help me?' asked Brian, breathing brandy fumes in all directions. 'I'm trying to trace a suitcase that I threw off the train at Banbury.'

'Not another bleeding wino!!' snapped the porter and slammed the shutter down. Having heard no more from that day to this, Brian assumes that *The Glums* were finally reunited with their luggage, or maybe at a later station someone threw *them* off the train.

Of course a story like Brian's told at the dinner table usually causes as chainreaction of tales from all parts of the globe, and to me they are always more entertaining and a great deal funnier than any jokes on the subject.

You know the type of set piece, going like:-

'The train now arriving at platforms 7, 8, 9 and 10 is coming in sideways.'

'Four returns, please.' 'Where to?' 'Back here you clown!'

'A return to Waterloo, please.' 'The station?' 'Yes – I'm a little late for the battle!'

Or - my own favourite, because I'd love to do it just once in my life. The train pulls into the station and a passenger who's been having a nap suddenly wakes, opens the window and shouts to a porter, 'Where are we?'

'Leatherhead!' comes the reply. 'Same to you, Pig-face,' yells the traveller and slams the window shut.

Ah – yes, each little gag has its own special worth, but none have the impact of tales like the late great Dr Runcie told.

It wasn't till I met the gentleman that I found he was a fellow scouser and possessed that wonderful Merseyside wit and wisdom. More importantly he as a brilliant talker, even on a one to one basis, and raconteur having that exquisite timing which some people are born with and others can never aspire to. An hour in his company was like five years of learning in any educational establishment and it was with awe and open mouth that I greeted each of his anecdotes, or antidotes as my late mother would have called them. Maybe she was right because they certainly cured the blues. Particularly the train story. Probably not 100% true, but then an archbishop must surely be allowed a little poetic licence.

Apparently it happened this way. The great man was traveling to Reading via London and was dressed in clerical mufti – basically a black suit with a dog-collar and very little regalia to state his rank. Having boarded a very crowded train he wandered up and down the corridor trying to find an empty seat. Finally he arrived at a compartment holding seven people and, excusing his intrusion, proceeded to squeeze himself in and hide behind a copy of the London Evening News. Off went the train and there sat a relaxed, if a little cramped, archbishop totally oblivious of his surroundings.

It seems, you see, that a mental institution from the Southern area had been on a trip to London to see the sights, and they were now returning to base. Little did the very reverend gentleman know that seven of them were sitting around him as he scanned the newsprint. All, though, was unceremoniously revealed to him at the first stop on the journey when suddenly the compartment door slid open and there stood a male nurse with a clip-board about to check on the passengers. As he pointed to each one he recognized he counted them off.

'One! Two! Three!…..' He paused at Doctor Runcie and said, 'Who are you?' 'I'm the Archbishop of Canterbury,' came the reply. 'Four!' said the nurse and carried on the count.

Great story – great man! Hope it was true, but who cares if not?

There's something about a train, be it steam, or diesel

or whatever, that lends an element of romance to a journey. Whether it's the result of the many films we've seen like 'Brief Encounter' or the many mysteries like 'Strangers on a Train', 'Murder on the Orient Express' and so on, but I always feel I'd love to hear the train, or at least the carriages, speak out about the wondrous happenings they have witnessed. The lives, the loves, the disasters, the reunions, the partings forever. What a film that would make! How sad that this will never come to pass but let us settle for our own humble experiences.

My own life has been criss-crossed with events, good or not, that happened on the railways of the world. Having only ever sampled the delights of the Liverpool overhead system in my early years it came as a bit of a culture shock to travel across Europe with a school summer trip. Our path led us from Dover through France and on into Italy, sampling the delights of railway stations along the route and sleeping on luggage racks with Boco McCann and several other reprobates.

It was my first, and almost my last, trip on a train being pulled by a diesel locomotive. Obviously everything appeared much cleaner because of the lack of smoke, but somehow the sound and feel of this modern upstart lacked the cheery rhythm that I'd become used to at home. Added to this was the fact that we were in the midst of a heatwave and the small compartment windows barely gave us enough air to breath. Water or indeed any form of liquid refreshment was at a premium. At each station (and there were many!) vendors would come aboard with buckets full of ice cubes, nestling in which were lusciously tempting Coca Cola and fizzy orange drinks. However, their purchase entailed a rather complicated palaver.

Still firmly assured of the stability of the great British pound, our elders had warned us not to carry lira (the currency low and getting lower) nor even French francs (no particular reason here), but rather we should stack up our sterling with small amounts of Swiss and Belgian francs. At the time Swiss francs were about four to the pound, whilst Belgian were around the one hundred and sixty mark. How pleasantly surprised we were then to find at one stop that our friendly neighbourhood vendor was charging the Swiss equivalent of four Belgian francs per bottle. Swiftly basic mathematics, prompted by greed, overcame all feeling of thirst and soon we were trading all our Belgian francs at about forty times their basic value. Lord knows what happened to the poor guy with the bucket of ice when he returned to base! C'est la vie, as they say!

But I mentioned that this venture abroad was nearly my last diesel-powered trip. Well, it came to pass, as it often does, that at the height of heatwaves and because of various other elemental factors, huge charges of electricity lurk in the atmosphere. This knowledge would have meant nothing to us nouveau riche money-changers even had we been forewarned. As it was, there was no warning at all - just huge rumbles of thunder and miles high cracks of lightning that seemed to rend the air. The train driver decided his safest port of call was a nearby freight yard, albeit surrounded by electricity pylons. Add this to a metal train on metal tracks and it would appear that he was asking for trouble.

We got it in the form of a thunderbolt which hit the train with such force that a couple of carriages were flung off the rails – even disturbing the slumbers of Tich Fallon, six foot six, seventeen stones, and the school shot-putter and champion sleeper. Tich had hardly been able to mutter, 'What the heck is happening?' (or words to that effect) when the door opened and our Geography master, Jim Preston, leaned in and screamed, 'We're all going to die boys, say your rosaries now!' before shuffling purple-faced along to the next compartment. We sat there the way stunned adolescents do when given the death penalty and waited for Mickey Kenyon to get the cigarettes out and pass them around. Somehow, with Heaven an immediate prospect, it didn't matter whether we were of smoking age or not. In fact it became so trivial that I got the Schnapps out and we had a guzzle of that. Not a bad way to spend our last minutes on earth, and probably no-one was more disappointed than us to live through it!

Still, a memorable trip with some unforgettable people. Jim Preston never quite had the same authority again, though, and his tales of derring do and valour in world War 2 were dismissed as the rantings of a coward. In fact, he became the subject of ridicule with such lines as 'Jim was in the SAS but he had to retire because his balaclava was too itchy.'

It's forty six years since those events and yet they remain as clear as crystal in my ageing mind. How clear must be the memories of the boys involved in the one school trip that I oversaw as a teacher. In the early seventies when engaged as deputy head and maths master at St Joan of Arc Secondary School in Bootle, I had a rush of blood and suggested to the Head that maybe a train journey to see the sights of London might be a good way of rewarding the better behaved pupils. I thought it would also help broaden their minds – little realizing how much my own mind would be broadened by the experience!

At the offset all was well, all boys agreeing to comply with my only condition that each must wear a grey top, be it shirt, sweater or jacket, so that I had at least a fighting chance of recognizing them from a distance. They'd all been advised on what type of packed lunch to bring and what games like chess, draughts or cards would keep them occupied particularly on the return journey when excitement had waned. Steaming South in fine sunny weather, all seemed to be going well and the Science master and I appeared to have complete control and not a care in the world. On arrival at Euston Station the boys disembarked in an orderly, in fact regimental, fashion and lined up in an almost straight line of twos, each displaying a distinctive grey top and awaiting orders.

You may not know that the trick of moving a body of youngsters is to place the best trusted at front and rear. The leaders are then given a point to move on to, a kerb or a particular shop, or pillar box. As the line crocodiles onward the teachers can then move up and down along the column bullying, chivvying or just talking the group along. Amazingly, this worked brilliantly and it was not long before we were all in a relaxed, even carefree, mood as we toured the British Museum, the Planetarium and, briefly, the Tower of London. At this point though the ambience of the whole experience overcame me totally and down came my guard for the one and only time and, at the speed of light, disaster beckoned.

Having thrilled at the good behaviour of my pupils I decided that an instant reward was due to them to impress the value of doing the right thing. So, unbelievably, I granted them a two hour period of total freedom on the strict understanding that all would present themselves at Euston Station in good time for the journey home, bearing in mind we were booked on the last train of the day. Off went the boys – thirty eight pairs of feet all apparently going in different directions, but at least still distinguishable through the grey tops and scouse accents.

Secretly I'd deputed ten of the older kids to oversee the general conduct and to dissuade any light-fingered child from temptation. So, safe in the knowledge that all the bases were covered, my fellow teacher and I repaired to a tea shop and enjoyed cream buns and strawberry jam. We puffed on a couple of cigarillos, and pretended to be business executives of distinction – men of the world, not schoolteachers, enjoying the world of Walter Mitty – if only for the day.

With surprising speed the clock went round the two hours in what felt like only ten minutes and we were on our way to Euston and the hoped for correct head count. And we almost got away with it. In fact, we were complete to all but two. Not a bad start, two missing out of thirty eight was no mean feat, especially with thirty minutes left before departure. And so we waited, and waited, and waited again. We waited for twenty minutes before desperation set in. Scouts were sent out and pupils were questioned. Then the decision was made that no-one would return if all could not return. Two missing meant thirty six stayed in London till they were found. Hardly had this knowledge been imparted to the group than, as if my magic, the two stragglers appeared with our scouts as escorts.

With sighs of relief all round I rechecked the numbers and we boarded the train and set off in jolly mood to while away the hours with games, or naps, or communal singing before being reunited with our loved ones. How idyllic it all was until, alighting at Lime Street Station, the Headmaster closely scrutinized each young face and then declared that 'two of these kids aren't ours.'

Gob-smacked I listened as he questioned the odd couple, and heard their distinct cockney voices. My God, what to do? What to say? In fact all I managed in the verbal department was, 'But - they're wearing grey tops!'

Too little too late. Very swiftly it became apparent what had happened. The Liverpool boys, eager to return home, and hampered by the fact that two of their number were adrift, had merely co-opted a pair of Londoners. So we were left with the awful problem of two of 'ours' loose in London and two of 'theirs' loose in Liverpool!

Happily all was resolved with the help of the Metropolitan Police and British Rail, bless their communal hearts. But on that day I learned another hard lesson about travelLing. Just as all that glitters is not gold, so all that wear grey tops are not essentially your own people. Always, I mean always, double check and even treble check your facts, your figures and your personnel.

This hard-earned knowledge served me in great stead many years later when I found myself in a totally different capacity as top of the bill in a touring show entertaining troops in what was then a divided Germany. We were part of a company called CSE – Combined Service Entertainment – and had travelled many miles across Western Germany to bring joy, or at least change, to the British forces. Having honed our skills on the various outlying bases – some of which could be five or six hours apart by road, we found ourselves heading for West Berlin and the final concert before brass hats and squaddies of many nationalities and unhindered by transport logistics.

We'd spent almost a week travelling by coach and observing a 40 mph maximum speed because we were being followed by the magician and his wife whose overladen truck (which was just marginally younger than Noah's Ark!) refused to go any faster. He blamed the weight of his budgies but we had our doubts! Suddenly we were all ensconced aboard a mighty looking diesel train, decked out with many different national flags and the whole shebang, twenty or so carriages, guarded by a single American soldier with what we later learned was an unloaded rifle.

As we thundered towards the border between East and West Germany we anxiously questioned our military escorts in an attempt to determine our security in a hostile land.

'Just say,' I ventured, 'that the Russians, in a fit of pique, decided to cross the border into the West. How long could the allies hold them?' 'Well .... ' drawled our young lieutenant guide, 'without nuclear weapons, about twenty minutes.'

This news was far from heart-warming and, together with the unarmed soldier, it made us feel just a little forlorn and not only eager to get to Berlin but double eager to get on, get off and get out as soon as possible.

It's at a moment like this that you don't need further discomfort but further discomfort is what we got. Just when you don't need an idiot, an idiot appears every time. And ours nearly cost us life, limb and liberty. In every band there is at least one lunatic and as a general rule of thumb he or she can be found in the ranks of drummers, guitarists or bass players. Our nutcase was from the latter. Dressed almost permanently in a black, full-length, down to the ankles leather overcoat and sporting those sinister rimless glasses the film baddies always wear, we nicknamed him 'KGB'. He looked so much like the archetypal secret service man, except that his behaviour was far too public and deranged to be of use to the spy agencies. Drop a serious musician enough times on his head and you will eventually produce our pal Tim – a fractured genius.

Admittedly we were all a little naïve about the day to day happenings in Germany and we certainly weren't ready for the over-enthusiastic search procedures at the border. Whilst allied soldiers made a cursory inspection of all trains leaving the West, the Russian forces virtually took the whole thing apart, supposedly looking for defectors from West to East – a very unlikely scenario. Just exactly who would want to break into East Germany we could not imagine. And just how they would accomplish it was beyond us. Hiding places on the train were few and liable to spot check searches by both sides. Hiding under the train was surely too hazardous, although many had apparently tried and succeeded when travelling East to West.

All these thoughts drifted through our minds but found no resting place. There we were on our way to a show and cared little or nothing for the problems of the Cold War. When I say 'we', however, I do not include 'KGB' whose entire morning was spent in working out how and where to hide beneath the train. And so, when we arrived at the checkpoint nutty Tim went into action. Leaving the compartment on the rail side of the train as the Russians entered from the platform side, he dropped down and attempted to secure himself amongst the pipes, struts and bogey wheels, not easy when wearing a head to toe leather overcoat. Hanging on for grim death and letting out the occasional grunt, to the eye of any onlooker our hero must have resembled an upside down cockroach. What he actually looked like, to the giant dog that found him, was another matter. Al I know is that when he was dragged to the platform he was short of a couple of chunks of body that he'd been born with.

Much, and I mean much, screaming shouting and whistle-blowing ensued and rifles and tommy guns were brandished all round. Red-faced police and soldiers screamed orders at no-one in particular and the not-so-bold-anymore Tim pleaded for his life, offered money for his life – even offered his luggage, bass guitar and amplifier for his life. None of this ever looked like working and in fact he would probably still be in custody if the rest of us hadn't urged the soldiers to 'shoot the prat now!' or 'lock him up forever pal!' or 'just leave him here tied to the lines and wait for a fast train to come along!'

Somehow this act of contra-pleading struck a nerve with the authorities who suddenly decided that their world would be a lot better if KGB stayed with us. And so, sadly, he was returned to us on the strict agreement that if he misbehaved again, one of the rest of us would suffer incarceration.

So from a lunatic who thought he could be clever let's move on to two extremely clever people who on occasions behaved like lunatics - with hilarious results!

Chapter 6

And... there's more!

Take any ventriloquist and put him or her amongst the public and you've got a joker who can't resist performing for free – sometimes to the point of irksomeness (is there such a word?).

Take any vent in the world except the best one in the world – Ray Alan. Ray, a legend in his time and his pal Lord Charles, have been recognized as the best of the best by all who know their onions – including Americans. And when the US says you're the best there can be no argument.

My friend Ray is one of the few exponents of the voice throwing art who doesn't grandstand just to appear to be flash. Wild horses would never drag him to the point of posing in public. Wild horses, no, but Johnny Walker whisky, maybe. Well certainly it did once, with side-splitting results.

It was this way... during a stint on the world cruise

of the P&O ship Canberra (more of which later in this book) when we docked at Yokohama harbour and Ray and I and our ladies caught the bullet train to Tokyo to see the sights and behave like tourists.

Safe-ish in the knowledge that hardly anyone who saw us would know us, we had possibly one or two more sips of booze than normal and proceeded to be silly. The devil was in us and memories of childhood pranks returned to spur our actions.

It all began with the four of us standing on a street corner and staring up at a large building, bodies and heads motionless - hands cupped over our eyes against any glare. Within minutes we had attracted a crowd of two dozen or more, all doing the same thing and continuing to do so as we slowly drifted off and left them!

Ha-ha we thought in our mischievous way - what a good opening jape. But what next? Talking to a pillar-box was always good for a laugh in the old days so we struggled to find the Japanese equivalent of the British postbox. It was at this point that the ladies decided it would be much funnier if, when talking to an object, the object responded with answers.

'Boing!' the bells rang and the light dawned. Ray, lovely Ray! The answer to the pranksters' collective prayer. Ray the genius gently weakened by the nectar of Bacchus and in that frivolous mood that makes grown men become little boys with wicked intent. We had the blueprint, we had the technology; now all we needed was the inanimate object -and then, behold, it was there before us. The ticket machine on Tokyo Station!

Quite similar to all vending machines world-wide it consisted of a narrow slit at the top for inserting coins, and a similar one at the bottom for ticket delivery. Ray chose to talk to the top one and then receive an answer by bending down and placing his ear to the bottom one, at the same time making answering noises without moving his lips or even one face muscle.

'How long have you been hiding in there?' he asked the top slit.

'Since 1944,' answered the bottom one.

'Well, it's safe to come out now; the war's over!' he assured the top.

'A likely story you Jap so and so!' snarled the bottom.

'Believe me mate, the war's been over for fifty years. Wait there and I'll go and get proof for you. I won't be long and you can talk to these Japanese folk till I come back,' was the last that Ray said, leaving the ever-growing crowd to take it in turns to speak into the higher slit, which in most cases meant a tip-toe stretch, and then to put an ear to the lower one requiring a jack-knife position.

With uncontrollable laughter and loud choruses of 'Bobbing up and down like this,' we naughty four boarded the train back to the ship and plotted further mayhem. It was not long in coming to mind. If the Japanese could fall for the gag, would the British?

Yes - we all agreed, providing there was an added incentive, and what better motive than greed, the most basic instinct of all.

Still flushed with success and still under the influence of alcohol, we boarded Canberra and made straight away to a bar to have one 'livener' before steering course to the Casino and its rows of slot machines – each propelled by the pulling of an upright lever, by a vast army of gamblers attempting to become rich upright citizens. There's something, isn't there, about winning a jackpot on a fruit machine that gives the feeling of robbing a bank?

So here we planned our latest escapade using the ventriloquial powers of Mr Alan and the hive of curiosity and greed of the average British onlooker.

Firstly we pumped several pounds worth of change into one of the beasts. This, naturally, registered as credits to be redeemed at any time by the pressing of a button. Next we attracted at least a little attention by chatting quite loudly about the gift that Roy had for talking to machines. Then, with half an ear from half a dozen bystanders, he began his spiel.

'Okay. This is Ray and I'm almost set to collect, OK?'

'Ready when you are Ray,' answered the machine.

'Right. Two more pulls and then the jackpot. All right with you?'

'Two more pulls it is,' came the reply.

Clunk! Went the first pull and three sluggy sounds meant nothing won.

Clunk - again, with the same result.

But, at the third pull Ray said, 'This is the one Jim!' - at the same time pressing the coin return button.

Three slugs were joined by the coughing up of eight or nine pounds worth of coins. Obviously we made a huge play of it and pretended the 'win' was more like fifty pounds and then scooped up the proceeds and trundled off leaving a room full of gaping passengers - some incredulous, some half on to the gag and quite a few suddenly shocked into sobriety. Next day we denied all knowledge of a 'talking machine' but, just for safety, the Ship's Captain barred all artistes from the casino with immediate effect.

Train stories are legion and are well worth the re-telling even more than once. What I find annoying is that no-one seems able to re-enact one as well as the original teller. And so, sadly, it is with my next journey into railway folk-lore.

Would that the master raconteur were with us to speak for himself but sadly we lost Roy Castle too young and too soon. How gifted was this humble, wonderful man, often in ways that very few know. Sure, we all think of him as a multi-instrumentalist, dancer, singer, presenter – you name it. But what about his skills as an actor, a top class comedian and ace talker, a man who could draw pictures with words, who could lead your mind upon a slow trip to happiness and contentment. Who cares if the stories weren't quite true, or even true at all. What we wanted was to hear the master tell them. And how well he did just that.

My particular favourite happened (or possibly not) on a packed commuter train entering London at about eight o'clock one dark, Friday, Winter's evening.

As we all know from bitter experience the worst type of carriage for this overworked service has got to be the non-corridor type which has a door on either side of the compartment for entry and exit from whichever way the platform appears. (And can't that be a mystery, right up until the last second?) Whilst leaving no scope for movement up or down the train it means that once you're aboard you're there until you debark.

So it was one Friday night that a train full of weary commuters bound for London suddenly (as they often do) slowed to a halt outside Clapham Junction, obviously waiting for the go-ahead signal. Three carriages from the front and oblivious to all and sundry a tired out, over-stressed, underpaid office junior was fast asleep and had been for twenty minutes or so. An air raid would not have roused him from his slumbers but, by that inexplicable twist of nature, the stopping of the train did.

Like a startled gazelle he opened his red rimmed eyes, heart pounding, looked at the seven fellow travellers and said, 'Clapham Junction?' Receiving a couple of nods of agreement he leapt to this feet, grabbed his briefcase, opened the left hand door and stepped out, falling flat on the track.

In that matter of three or four seconds before reality replaces fantasy the gob-smacked passengers stared at the open door from whence our poor unfortunate had stepped into the abyss. Before any of them could speak or even react, the briefcase that had spearheaded the exit from the train was thrown back in by a hand dripping blood. This was quickly followed by a totally dishevelled office junior, bleeding from one or two more prominent places, particularly the nose, and covered in that dusty grime that only lies on railway tracks.

'I'm so sorry,' muttered Mr Grimey. 'You must think I'm a complete idiot.' And before any or all could agree, he shuffled across the compartment, opened the right hand door and stepped out, falling out on to the track again.

History does not recall (nor could Roy) whether the ultimate indignity was that the train moved on, leaving him face down on the track. It would be a cruel ending, but then life has to be cruel to be funny sometimes. The trick surely is to use all circumstances and adversities to one's own advantage. Make the most of the cards that life deals because, as the man once said, 'Every hand's a winner, just like every hand's a loser.'

How much better it is to triumph against all the odds, than to win with an easy ride. How great the satisfaction of knowing you have made it because of your own efforts – OK with a little luck thrown in on the way. Here we pause for a second to remember that, as a rule when travelling, we must always and ever keep an open mind, be flexible, stand ready to adapt our plans and our goals to suit the prevailing conditions.

I was long a fan of Clive Brandy and his outrageous antics. Deeds he did have gone down in showbusiness folk-lore. Others have tried to take credit for the doings and failed. Others have tried to re-enact his exploits only to meet with disastrous results. When I knew the legend he was married to that wonderful singer Iris Williams and served as her mentor, manager, driver, producer – you name it he did it, including organizing fish, chips and mushy peas suppers.

However, my favourite tale of the late lamented Clive happened well before I met him and, not only is tantamount to being unbelievable, but gives us yet another lesson to learn when preparing to be fit to travel. The whole episode began and ended in Britain. But it's the bit in the middle that is most interesting.

Clive, a would-be comedian and raconteur, had risen from driver to manager of a well-known British singer and had arranged a tour of Australia for his star. At the time, the late 60s, Australia was still a vast and partly untapped source of revenue for entertainers and many a million was made by those acts who could perform *on* stage and keep their heads and their manners *off* it.

Such, sadly, was not the case with Clive's act. A man of mighty physical presence and resonant voice, but a man liable to go off at a tangent with backstage behaviour and become an alcohol-fuelled loose cannon. This particular trait Clive hoped to quench by making the tour as busy as possible with venues and media gatherings, constant travel and self-imposed discipline. And so it seemed to be for about two weeks - and then the rot set in.

During one night off a minor exchange of words, a petulant sulk and the star was gone. Not gone out of the hotel, but gone to who knows where, leaving Mr Brandy, as he later remarked, 'Jobless, starless and potless!' But, not to worry. Of such calamities is made the stuff of heroes and legends. And so it proved to be.

Happily the whole affair happened in such a great country as Australia where the future is wide open to those who'll work hard for it. And work hard was Brandy's by-word. Firstly trying his luck as a touring comedian, visiting stock yards and out-of-the-way theatres and clubs and dying the death in every one. 'Too corny, too clean and too English!' was one of his better write-ups, and soon even Brave Heart himself realized he'd have to think again. So, if the brain and wit failed in this land of plenty, then the brawn must prevail and Clive had plenty of it. Using his stamina, boundless energy and general bonhomie he fast became a regular worker at the stock yards, lumber camps and all points east.

Unknown to his compadres though the whole time he worked, young Brandy had but one dream in mind; to reach Sydney and the sea, board a ship and work his passage home to Blighty and to gawd knows what the future might hold. And this he did, returning to the east coast a sadder, wiser, but fitter man than when he'd last left it. After some wrangling Clive talked his way aboard a freighter which was bound for Southampton and subsequently served as a seafaring dogsbody to pay for his passage.

Disembarking back in jolly old England, his next move was to head for London bearing in mind he was, as he so rightly explained, 'potless.' Nonetheless he played the old ace in the hole of the penniless traveller.

He found a discarded platform ticket and passed the ticket collector in the guise of a relative or friend seeing off a loved one. Once on the platform it became twice on to the train, and in a trice in a carriage and seated. The London train pulled out and, instead of relaxing, the bold Brandy sat and dreamed of the ultimate accolade for any traveller.

'If I can get off this train in London without paying, I'll have come half-way round the world for nothing!' Now there's a world record that John Kenny the lunatic cyclist would be proud of!

But what to do and how to do it? Well, there is an old tale of deeds performed on crowded trains, particularly during the war and Clive knew the tale well.

Wait for the train to travel half an hour or so and gamble that someone eventually will use the toilet. Stationing one's self outside the toilet area and allowing a gap of say six seconds for the 'victim' to be seated, the idea was to bang on the loo door a la ticket collector, and bellow, 'Tickets please!'

This invariably resulted in a ticket being shoved under the door for inspection. This is exactly what the bold Brandy did, acquiring a bona fide right of passage and achieving a minor world record in the process.

For those who look for lessons in every story please remember, dear traveller, that you never surrender your ticket to a stranger, most especially one on the other side of a toilet door.

So it seems I have led you on a long and oft-convoluted path whilst trying to cram in advice and 'almost true' events that may or may not have been so. Safe to say that if you, like me, love trains and railways and all their fantastic history then you'll allow a little poetic licence.

It's a far cry for me from the Blackpool Belle, a fabulous old train that ran a service to the seaside Mecca of the north, packed with kids on a Saturday night – teenagers out for anything and everything they could find in the way of entertainment and romance.

Ah, the dreams that were made and hearts that were broken as we thundered across Lancashire in search of Eden, but invariably found only Stockport and the like. It was a time when the railways meant escape from boredom and drab streets and little or nothing to do. Its only importance was to help relieve us teenagers from the reality of life in the 50s. We had the Blackpool Belle on land and the Royal Iris on water. The Royal Iris is a pleasure boat on the Mersey – much more of which later.

In those days we never realized or cared about the downside of rail travel. Who of us ever thought or cared about the people of Runcorn – that garden spot which features amongst its other charms a railway bridge across the Mersey. Yes, who indeed ever bothered to look into the downside of the structure. The fact that trains would thunder across it at various intervals did nothing to disturb the sleep of 99% of Great Britain. But to the good folk of Runcorn and its environs the railway came to loom large in its heritage – particularly the early morning train which was blamed totally for the rise in the local birth rate.

'You see ...' explained a hardened resident, 'It clatters through at a hell of a rate and wakes up all and sundry.'

'Shame!' I said.

'But worse still ...' he went on, 'It wakes people too early for work and too late to go back to sleep, and so the inevitable happens!'

I must admit this conversation took place before 24 hour television and Sky digital, but who knows it may still apply. Maybe Runcorn could replace China as the home of the world's greatest birth rate increase.

And so, with special thanks to all the story tellers

who've shared their rail travel with me, and still mindful of many more modes of travel to documentate, I sadly have to wind up this section of the book.

Like you, I'm sure I still get that special buzz from 'riding the rails'. I close my eyes and think of a trip to the Blue Mountains near Sydney, Australia, aboard the only double deck train I'd ever seen. A wonderful journey, a memorable journey. Just like the Orient Express! How I'd love to travel its full distance across Europe and back. Ah yes, the splendour it brings to mind! The romance, the possible intrigue, the feeling of being an international traveller, thereby receiving an extra furrow on the brow as an emblem of rank and experience.

Ah yes, all these and many more thoughts race through my mind as I decide to 'pay off' this wee discourse on the glories of rails and trains. And so it is that I leave you with two tales, almost legendary now, certainly less romantic than the Blue Mountains or the Orient Express and, possibly, just possibly more believable than Roy Castle's! Sorry Roy, never doubted you my friend, but for real drama and excitement aboard a moving vehicle try these two from the sunny North of Britain.

Picture a crowded train heading from Scotland towards London on a particularly slow day - meeting hold-ups, track repairs and all things nasty. Somewhere aboard is a thirty-something salesman who, accompanied by his charming spouse, is to attend an interview which could alter his life and his job prospects for all time. Having been greeted by the dulcet tones of the friendly neighbourhood train guard with his update of weather, timings and apologies for delay, it suddenly became apparent that, barring elephants on the line, they were within an hour of their destination.

Up jumped our would-be nouveau riche executive and, shaving bag in hand and watched by the other seven passengers, he stepped and stooped his way to the door, declaring to his good lady, 'I think I'll just go and freshen up.'

Off he strode, looking resplendent in his pink golf shirt and pale blue slacks. Having reached the toilet and having locked himself in, he filled the sink with hot water and lathered his face for shaving. As he prepared the safety razor the train suddenly lurched over a particularly bumpy stretch of track and the soapy water in the sink swilled over his previously immaculate trousers. In his instinctive reaction to the jolt he fell forward banging his head on one of five silver screw heads on the mirror. This raised a huge lump on his otherwise furrow-free forehead. Deciding to press on regardless he raised the safety razor to his cheek just as the train lurched again. This caused the razor blade to slide uncontrolled down his face leaving a slash an inch and a half long and almost as deep!

Making the best of everything with the use of that toilet tissue that was really thin cardboard and was only ever supplied to British Rail he began to pack his gear away when there was a fierce banging on the toilet door.

'Come on mate, I'm bursting here!' bellowed a very agitated passenger. Sadly, our businessman unlocked the door just as Mr Impatient outside put his shoulder to it. The result was the hundred miles an hour opening of the door, which then crashed into our hero's nose causing it to pump blood at a virtually unstoppable rate. Further use of the toilet paper only succeeded in smearing the blood all over his face and shirt collar.

Resigned to his fate, and frightened to check his appearance in the mirror, 'Mr Pink (and red) shirt' shuffled back to his compartment. Bearing in mind he'd left in a blaze of eagerness and with the words, 'I think I'll go and freshen up,' he now returned looking anything but fresh. Huge blue lump on the forehead, still throbbing from the impact of the screw head, long gash on the cheek, nose stuffed with blood-soaked tissue, trousers and shirt soaked in soapy water, he regained his seat, stared at his horror-stricken wife and said, 'That's better!'

Thereby lies the tale of a man whose entire future was jeopardized and possibly destroyed by the fates ganging up on him and taking him from one level down to another with no sign of help on the way. How often, though, do we find all manner of help being given and this in itself ruining someone's day.

I've always been a fan of the train guards' announcements both before, during and after a journey. How witty these people can be and how vital sometimes is the information they give. How much stress they ease and how much better they make passengers feel; we'd be lost without them. To those who don't believe my words I say, 'Check what used to happen to vulnerable innocents before the upgrade of customer care out there in the wide, wide world and possibly a little nearer to us than we think. There is at least one man who would have given his eyeteeth for the answer to one vitally important question .... 'Did his train stop at Crewe?'

Here is the story in a nutshell, bearing in mind the first rule of travel – check all details major and minor before setting off. A shortish, thinnish, fiftyish chap boarded a south-bound train at Liverpool Lime Street, heading for his day of destiny. If his meeting down the line was successful he would be richer by at least £100,000 as the result of a shipping deal between his one- man company and a huge multi-national importer. All he needed to do was to appear, sign the document before 4.00pm and the world, as they say, would be his oyster. The fact that the oyster snapped shut before he grasped the pearl is purely due to bad planning, bad luck and bad choice of bedfellow.

Seated opposite our smallish entrepeneur was a large-ish, in fact outsize-ish, gent of more than six feet in height and certainly the same in girth - a powerful man with a friendly smile and a relaxed demeanour. What better person to share forty minutes or so with while trundling towards your ultimate destiny?

As the usual banter about weather, sport and all things mundane gradually petered out, our small friend asked, quite innocently, 'Any idea what time this train stops at Crewe today?'

'Oh heck,' replied the big fellow. 'It's Wednesday and this train doesn't stop at Crewe on Wednesdays. It goes through Crewe, straight on non-stop to Euston.'

'No – it's got to stop at Crewe,' spluttered the little fellow.

'Sorry old son,' sighed his companion, 'On Wednesdays it's straight through Crewe.'

'But it's a matter of life or death that I get off at Crewe,' sobbed Mr Small.

'Well, look mate,' assured Mr Big, 'The train doesn't stop at Crewe but it does slow right down as the platform bends. Why don't I hold you out the window, you get your legs going in a running mode and I'll drop you?'

'Will you?' smiled the wee man.

'Sure. No problem!' said the big fellow, 'Just relax now and leave it to me.'

So twenty or so minutes went by and the train started its approach to Crewe Station.

'All set?' asked the big 'un.

'Ready when you are,' beamed the little 'un, and he was hoisted out of the window and held suspended by his mighty strong companion.

'Got your legs going?'

'Yes – they're going like the clappers!'

'OK – I'm dropping after the count of three. Good luck! One – two – three!!'

Down plunged our little chum, his feet hitting the platform in perfect rhythm and carrying him along for ten or fifteen yards by sheer momentum. However, just as he began to think of applying the brakes he felt a huge pair of hands grabbing him under the armpits and hoisting him back in the air

.'Blimey mate,' said a deep, gruff voice as he was hauled back aboard. 'You were lucky I spotted you or you'd have missed this train!!'

No deal done, no future changed forever, no happy ending except for we who share the comic moment.

Chapter 7

Ferry nice

Travel may, or may not, broaden the mind but cruising can certainly broaden the beam!

I suppose our communal first memories of life at sea would centre around films, TV series' like 'The Love Boat' or holiday programmes where everyone wishes they were somewhere or other. But, in practice, how do they measure up to our true-life experiences of the ocean and its romantic splendour?

Probably a good percentage of us would have to admit that the dream is often far more glamorous than the reality but then isn't that the case with everything in the world – including ourselves?

How often have we admired our own reflection in a full-length mirror, little knowing how, or if, we impress other people who see us through a different eye? So – let's put away the rose-tinted glasses and look at, and take, the world of sea travel at its face value.

Let's enjoy the fun, the adventure, yes and even the romance of a trip like no other – adrift across an endless ocean where tomorrow is just like today and all cares of the outside world are too far away to worry about. Wouldn't it be heaven to have that life all the time? And there are people who do. But, would you believe it? They get bored!

In fact, in many cases it's the actual change from normality which can lighten up a day. Minor disasters of the funny kind can actually produce fonder and longer memories than the idyllic moonlight nights of tropical splendour.

And so, dear reader, it is with this in mind that I launch myself (no pun intended!) into the arena of sea travel with its myths, legends and apochryphal stories.

In my own case it all began in the most basic manner with trips on the Liverpool ferries to New Brighton and back – literally a ferry across the Mersey. For an hour or two it was a chance for youngsters to live the life of the legendary sea-dogs like Captain Blood who, like us, strode the decks whilst others did the work.

How like pirates we felt as we headed towards the Wirral and the delights of New Brighton beach and funfair. How we enjoyed the sun on our backs (Do you remember those days when the sun shone all the time and it never ever rained? No? Neither do I, but back to the plot) and the wind in our hair! How easy it was, or so we thought, to be a real sailor – a cake-walk in fact. So easy we thought that there surely was nothing to the sea-faring profession. No gales, no rough seas, no seasickness. Ah – heady days – gone all too soon!

My sea-going eyes were first opened when travelling across the Irish Sea on the Liverpool to Dublin ferry, a source of great entertainment in my youth with accordions playing and people on open decks singing and quaffing Guinness – 'the food' as the Irish called it.

Being young and very impressionable it seemed to

be the perfect life for me – that was until we left the shelter of the Mersey bar and hit a minor storm which scattered the singers mostly to the rail to be sick and silenced all instruments for the rest of the trip.

Having experienced roughish weather whenever we sailed to Ireland it seemed that I would never be able to see any fun in the journey but, as years went by, and sea-legs became steadier it was possible to relax and enjoy the sillier side.

Take the almost classic story of the racegoers travelling from Dublin to Liverpool to watch the Grand National race at Aintree. Of course those of us who have merely watched ferries arrive and leave, and those who have boarded or alighted in groups following the leader will not know that there are certain rules to ferry travel; in particular to counter the modern day terrorism outbreaks there has to be one specific gangplank for the seamen to use. This is usually clearly marked so that even a blind man can see.

Of course, that doesn't always apply to a man who's blind drunk. And such was the case on this particular day when a band of Irish Buckoes, well-lubricated and adrift from all the other passengers, began to climb the sailors' gangplank.

'Hoi!' shouted a deck officer, 'You can't come up there!'

'Whoi?' enquired the leading lush.

'That gangplang is crew only!'

'Is it indeed? Then which one is Holyhead?'

Obviously, for the rest of his life he would argue that ferries do go to Crewe – even if it is landlocked!

I suppose it's easy to scoff at such behaviour when looking back with a wealth of experience, but surely we've all made mistakes in the travel department that could have been laughable to others.

Look at me. For years my only taste of the delights of sailing came from trips aboard the Royal Iris – a Mersey ferry that was geared up for fun. Bands played in a couple of ballrooms; bars dispensed all manner of brews; boys and girls of the teenage variety danced and rocked the night (or a good part of it!) away and guess what sustained us in the food category? Why – the food that gave the vessel its lifetime nickname – 'the floating fish and chip shop!'

There I looked for romance – sometimes too desperately. There I longed to be for all eternity, happy to let the world's problems and even my call-up for National Service, pass me by. Deep down I knew it could never be and it never was. And I might say that it would be a longish time before I again would put to sea. It would be as a married man and a man bowed down by hard work as a schoolteacher by day and entertainer by night.

Yes, in the bones of one so careworn and world weary there lay the spirit of adventure and freedom that demanded that I take a 'trip to Fairyland.'

Such was the title of a holiday advertised in a national paper in the early sixties and beautifully illustrated with a sleek liner cruising on a glass smooth sea and sporting lots of jolly passengers waving from each deck. The reality, however, was somewhat different.

'Four days at sea in a floating paradise,' was in actual fact one day boarding, one day disembarking and three nights and two days travelling to Norway with a stop for a couple of hours. Alas, you see, our sleek liner was basically a ferry loaded with cars, skiers and Norwegians, all heading for Bergen as fast as they could go. The only 'trippers to Fairyland' were four British couples who had read the ad and succumbed.

Too late we found that we had walked into the trap. Too late we realized that, leaving Newcastle at deadish of night was not quite the norm for an exotic cruise. Too late, too late .... Yeah, verily too late for everything!

Me being only a teacher of mathematics I had a built-in excuse for not knowing what might be ahead. But my wife, a geography major, should have been able to give me at least a hint of the rough weather to come. But no – no hint, not even a glimmer, and so I blithely entered our small-to-miniscule cabin and opted for the upper bunk. Not the best place for a seasick wretch but then who expected weather rougher than in the press ad?

Unphased by the fact that the sink in the cabin folded in and out to save space and the fact that to undress in comfort one person had to lie on a bunk or go outside, we sat and decided that we could cope, despite being on a deck full of children who ran riot at all times of the day and night. Some holiday for a pair of teachers!

Still, the first night was spent on a calm sea and in the company of our six country folk who, with true British aplomb, had decided to make the most of things. Each had tales to tell and most were of the happy times and better days. Only one brought an element of doubt to the mind and that was an ex-soldier who had apparently travelled by transport to Bergen in the war and was 'almost certain that the North Sea weather was rough and the winds up to gale force, although I might be wrong.'

He wasn't. Days one and two were fairly settled weatherwise and the odd glass of port and brandy banished all thoughts of Mal de Mer. But that was only going there!

In Norway we unloaded all the kids and skiers and had the ship totally to ourselves – we eight stalwart

Brits. Or so it was at first! Then, like the book, 'Ten Little Indians' we slowly diminished in number and enthusiasm but that would be sixteen hours into the future. Right now we indulged ourselves in all foods and many forms of alcoholic beverage intent on making this the party of a lifetime – in truth it almost was because the resultant fall-out was nearly the death of most of us.

All night we partied – eating and drinking whatever came to mind, or more truthfully to hand! Nordic beers and liquors washed down all manner of food - reindeer meat and such delicacies. None gave a thought about tomorrow except the ex-soldier who'd 'been here before and know the ins and outs, mate!'

He alone insisted on eating only British-type grub. This consisted of the Bergen version of roast beef and Yorkshire pud – although cooked in a way he'd never experienced before.

Nonetheless the festivities went on and we gallant souls plunged happily into the night unaware, like babes in the wood, of what might befall us tomorrow. Many a tale was told and many an unaccompanied song was sung. Ah – the happy times, times to last forever. May these be the worst of our days!

Having laughed and caroused in such wonderful surroundings who cared if we died tomorrow. None of us did. But we should have because tomorrow was almost nigh and the heaven of carefree Dr Jekyll was about to become the hell of Mr Hyde.

The morning broke as lots do, bright and clear, wind-free and beautiful to behold. The day promised much in the way of ideal sailing conditions but then what did we know? A warning shot, literally across our bows, should have been the words of the steward as we joined the Smorgasbord open breakfast.

'Always remember,' he said in almost perfect English, 'The best cure for seasickness is what you see all around you – land!!'

In retrospect I realized that he was warning us that we were still in the comfort and shelter of the harbour and would not know the full consequences until we sailed. But retrospect is retrospect and here and now is what is important to the ignorant and so we allowed stomachs to overrule heads and tucked into the massive breakfast feast.

Fuelled by a pleasant evening in port and a good night's sleep we travellers to Fairyland partook of every dish there was to taste – bacon, egg, and all things British – fish, cold meats, cheeses and all things Continental.

I lost count of the platefuls I consumed and the order in which I consumed them. What I do know is that I finished it all off with a small plate of curried rabbit and rice, washed down with very strong coffee.

Then, full of the joys of Spring and breakfast fare I wandered to the front of the ship, chose a deck chair and slumped ungracefully down to have a nap and to soak up the sun's rays. 'Ah – this is the life!' thought I, 'Who cares what the poor people are doing!'

And there I lay or, more specifically, lolled about, while the effects of an oversized multi-national meal waved over me. I probably would have stayed there forever had it not been for the clanking. Clanking? – Yes, clanking.

That was the only description of the noise that woke me up. A steady clank, swish, clank and a feeling of regular, if jerky, movements. What could it be? Was I being transported to heaven in some form of metal container which had developed a lurch of its own? Was I gliding through eternity on rusty wheels? No – oh dear, no!

Heaven was nowhere in sight nor in prospect. The opposite was in fact the case. Hell beckoned at an alarming rate. But why? And, more importantly, how? Whatever the answer it involved coldness and getting wet, wet off and on like being caught by the spurts of a water-sprayer in a park or garden. Gradually, curiosity overtook sleepiness and I opened my eyes, albeit slowly and one at a time. Now, and only now, did the full truth make itself known to me. I was alone and adrift on the deck, totally abandoned by wife and friends, sliding around in a sunchair, which was literally chained to the deck, which accounted for the clanking. The cold and wetness came from the spray and biting air of the North Sea as the ship crashed into a force ten gale with only myself above decks.

Where were the others? Had they perished? Was I now a widower? Was I the only survivor? Not a bit of it. In fact I was the only mug who hadn't returned to warmer climes like the bar or restaurant. All had fled the cruel sea, including my wife and no-one had given a thought for the poor marooned soul strapped down to the deck and held firmly in place by a stomach full of curried rabbit and rice! Full that was, until the swirling of the ship reached my brain and gave forth the realisation that shortly, very shortly, I would need to offload my entire breakfast and possibly yesterday's lunch and dinner.

Yes, indeed, these were critical times. Too late, much too late for a stabilizing glass of port and brandy. Too late for Quells or jabs from the doctor. In fact, almost too late to reach a shipboard loo and sink to my knees burying my head in the traditional fashion that is adopted by all who have overimbibed or, in my case, been totally abandoned.

To this day I can still recall the croaking voice which

apparently was mine, repeating those oft-used words, 'Never again! Never again!'

Ah – but never is a long, long time and, 'again and again' is the more likely outcome of such folly. It certainly was in my case.

Chapter 8

There - and back

Needless to say, it was quite a long time before I ventured seaward again and I've never even attempted to stare curried rabbit in the face again. But – times change and needs must and the world still goes around.

In the early 70s I was offered a trip on a proper cruise liner, the deal being that I did two or three shows and, in return, could take Pat on a ten day break in the sun. (No mention of the Bay of Biscay and the possibility of gale- force winds!) No warning of how sun, sea and sangria can affect even the most resolute brain. Looking back thirty-odd years I'm amazed at how naïve we both were. Starry-eyed and impressionable! Ready to accept all the blurb - both written and verbal – about the wonders of cruising. How could we have taken so long to discover its splendour? How come nobody had recommended it to us before? Were we the only ones in Bootle, and possibly Britain, who had never partaken of the beauties of this form of travel?

Well, from personal experience, I'm here to untangle

the myth and give you my unbiased list of the pros and cons – more pros I might stress – of life at sea. But I've drifted from the point and so let me return to the early 70s and the good ship Ithica.

She was a Greek registered ship of fine lines and more than able crew, playing host to about five hundred British passengers looking forward to a journey to the Canary Islands and the Mediterranean.

Having made a couple of appearances on the TV series 'Comedians' and feeling confident to the point of cockiness I had made a comedy LP record and sold copies at every venue. Pat decided that everybody on such a pleasure trip would buy a copy as a souvenir. In fact she estimated that they'd buy two each – one for a friend or relative. So – we dragged a trunk filled with one thousand LPs aboard our floating hotel, unpacked all the bags and joined our fellow travellers on a shipboard tour.

It's easy now to see how the apocryphal stories of life at sea have come about. Just listening to people's immediate reaction to events is meat and drink to the comic mind:-

'What's that noise?'

'They've just dropped the anchor.'

'I'm not surprised – it's been hanging over the side all day!'

'Just look at all that vast expanse of water.'

'Yes – and that's only the top!'

'Captain – how high is that funnel?'

'About ninety feet sir. If you like we can take you up to the top in a bosun's chair.'

'Sorry, mate, but I wouldn't go up there in a three-piece suite!'

What was not evident as we mingled and chatted

was the steady movement of the ship. Not just up and down as she met the rippling waters, but side to side as well – and at the same time!

Nothing untoward, but possibly just a little niggling nudge to the brain of the possibility of things to come if and when the wind blew and the seas rose. And rise they did! Boy, did they! And, as in all things, the timing was immaculate

Literally, just as I was preparing to go on stage for my first show, the Ithica entered the Bay of Biscay and hit a force 10 gale which pitched and rolled the ship thither and yon. Looking into the auditorium from backstage I noticed what I took to be strawberry punnets on each empty seat. Little did I know that these little baskets were for the use of anybody who felt seasick.

It soon became evident when I launched myself on stage and attempted to be funny whilst clinging steadfastly to a microphone stand and the piano. As the pummelling of the sea increased up came the 'punnets' for the people to be sick in. This, of course, brought out the worst in my digestive tract and suddenly I was heaving along with the others.

Not even the affect of nervous tension and adrenalin, which we in the business call 'Doctor Footlights' could help and soon I became so wretched that there was nothing else for me to do but mumble an apology to the heaving masses and run for the nearest sink or toilet.

Years later I was able to laugh at the event and, in fact, highlight my act with an apochrophyl, but almost surely true, story of the entertainer who found himself in a similar position to myself.

Having launched himself on to the stage in a gale, he proceeded to relaunch himself off again in a frantic struggle to regain the safety of his cabin, a sink, a toilet and possible a port and brandy if he could keep it down. In his haste, though, he forgot the first rule of the sea – 'When you're ill on a ship they hide your cabin!!' This sentence is writ large in the annals of maritime history and should never be ignored. But ignore it our hero did and on and on he sprinted in the vain hope of sanctuary. Thus, it was that, as he crashed and banged his way along another unrecognizable corridor, (sorry – 'gangway') a cabin door opened and out stepped a lady wearing nought but a startled look. She'd thought she was going to her bathroom but had opened the wrong door and was out in he passageway. As the poor dear attempted to shrivel up ball-like, and try to cover her embarrassment with both arms she said plaintively, 'I'm so ashamed; I'm sorry.'

'Don't worry, love,' muttered the unwell 'turn' 'I'm not going to live long enough to tell anyone!'

Ah yes – a story well worth the retelling and but a faint scratch on the surface of travellers' tales. Someone should write a book (not me, please!) on the dos and don'ts of life at sea.

I always think the don'ts would loom larger than the dos but all could be resolved by remembering the golden rule of life itself – 'When in doubt, definitely don't!!'

How that phrase could have saved us all a deal of grief in past times. No need for ten commandments when that one piece of sound advice is adhered to. Oh yes, I hear you say, it's easy in retrospect and indeed it is. But life wouldn't be half as amusing if we lived in a land of retrospect. There'd be no calamities, no 'never agains' and for my wife there'd be no wine tastings in the Canaries.

The portents were not good from the very beginning. The Ithica pitching and rolling, my sudden bout of sea sickness in 'The Bay' and then the almost instant calmness as we hit better weather and wondered why we'd ever felt so queasy. And then, like a beacon in the darkness, appeared the beautiful Isle of Madeira – serene and sun-drenched – the ultimate cure for the blues. And, moreover, the promise of great fun ashore and many sights to be seen.

Yes, Madeira would put right all that was wrong with us and herald the new beginning. But wait – where to start? So many things to do and see, but in which order. Surely that would be important. And so it proved. And luckily we got the order right first time.

As on all cruise ships there is a thriving tour department looking after all trips ashore and sight-seeing activities and as a firm tip to one traveller it is always worth listening to port lecturers and tour staff when preparing to sally forth to places unknown.

Too often the unwary traveller takes heed of the so-called expert veteran cruisers who've been there and done all that and who never believe in planning.

It's safer for you and me to treat these folk with suspicion and go for safety to the paid and well-researched members of the Ship's Company for advice.

So it was for us when we attended the tour lecture and watched the film of the beautiful scenery, the splendid vineyards, the endless fine restaurants, the wine-tasting and the basket run. Oh yes – the basket run. San Francisco has its cable cars, Sydney has its opera house and Madeira has its basket run - more like a semi-controlled toboggan run really, but at times far more exciting (that's putting it mildly!)

The course for this downhill charge runs through endless streets of cobbled stones worn smooth by the constant flow of baskets full of camera-wielding sightseers gaudily dressed in obscenely coloured shorts, tops, socks and hats and trying desperately to mingle in with the locals and losing – if only on the grounds of red faces and arms compared with brown! The early part of the adventure appears somewhat tame when the basket is dragged uphill to the starting point. It was at this point in our own particular jaunt that I began to suspect that all was not completely well with our 'driver'.

The driver is the man who's totally in charge of propulsion and steering of a wickerwork box containing two healthily built foreigners who have no common language with him, but who, when they see the full gamut of the downhill run are already blessing his name and wishing him health and strength of body and mind - at least till they reach the bottom.

In my case my prayers were all the more fervent when I realized that 'Charlie' - funny name for a Madeiran – appeared to have some type of asthmatic complaint which resulted in a most disturbing wheezing and coughing – even when walking normally on the flat. Boy, how that sound multiplied when we hurtled downhill and around corners, almost uncontrollably, as Charlie attempted to hang on with his eight stones against the combined total of twenty stones of us and the basket.

All seemed to be a blur of shiny cobbles, other travellers applauding, young girls attempting to hand us small flowers, and houses and people going by at a blistering rate of knots - all accompanied by coughing, wheezing, deep rasping intakes of air and faint appeals to 'Madre Mio' and various other members of the celestial choir.

Whose prayers prevailed we shall never know but we eventually slithered to a safe halt at the bottom of the hill, looking and feeling like something the cat had dragged in. Glad that we'd had the smiling photograph taken at the start of the ride because we couldn't raise the energy at the finish, and vowing to repay the Lord in kind very soon, we took our leave of Charlie, heaving and hawking and unbelievably attempting to light a cigarette!

Ah well – you can always expect one stunning experience when touring. Can you? Did I say one? Hold on – let me rethink and let me recount ....

Managing to stay alive on a downhill toboggan run is probably all that one person would desire in any one day but on my day ashore this was only the beginning. It was still only mid-morning and the couriers were in fine fettle mustering the troops for our next stop – the wine-tasting.

Amazing, isn't it, how many people, serious non-wine drinkers, can be drawn to an event when told that the drink is free? I'm told that there had been a special wine-tasting cruise aboard Ithica hosted by the Sunday Times newspaper. Whatever and wherever it did and went, the organizers thought it a good idea to test the passengers on the knowledge they had gained over the two-week run up and down the Med.

Apparently the highest score out of 50 was 2!! Ah – the signs and portents of disaster were already there to see if only we'd taken the trouble!

They say that strange things happen at sea, but even stranger can happen on land – especially to me.

Pat and I had teamed up with a charming lady, a widow, and her two daughters (thirteen and sixteen) and followed the throng towards the cobbled area of town and the tables laden with wine glasses – all full and of many different brews.

'The trick is to sip the wine, let it tickle the pallet and then spit it out,' recommended our guide.

'Rhubarb!' thought the mass of British flesh being squeezed towards the alcoholic display.

'Try to remember which numbers you prefer for reference when buying,' went on our guide.

'Try and get us to remember our names when we're finished!' I thought to myself.

And so it came to pass that we happy band of pilgrims forever destined to travel the world in search of freedom and enlightenment, joined the crocodile queue of participants in the Madeira wine-tasting.

Pat and her new found friend, Anne, led the way for our battalion, sipping, half-gargling and spitting out. That procedure, in fact, lasted for three consecutive wines, one more than I honestly expected myself. Then the whole shebang began to unravel. It's hard to say who swallowed first but the result was immediate.

'I like this one I think,' said one.

'I'm not so sure. Let's try the previous one again,' said another.

'No – let's leave that till we've done all the others,' added a third.

'Done all the others?' 'Done all the others?' How easily the uninitiated can pick up the language and jargon of the wine guru!

This conversation and its like went on for the neck-end of twenty minutes before the total effects became apparent. Slowly the chat became slurring and the reasoning became unreasonable.

'Was it eleven or six we drank after four?'

'When?'

'You know.'

'Oh, yearh.'

So it went on more and more 'tastings' leading to more and more swallowings and less and less sense being talked.

Eventually alcohol and gravity began to take over and slurring of speech became sinking of bodies and loss of all senses.

And so, exit three (or was it three dozen?) well-satisfied tasters who would take no further part in the proceedings of the day. Or, in fact, of the next, nor the day after that!

Three days of oblivion beckoned but, as yet, we who were able to see could not see it coming. In my own case I was just happy to reach our cabin – a tipsy lady under each arm. Pat and Anne, the new muppets, safe and sound in the arms of oblivion, and desposited on a bed each - there to lie for over forty-eight hours, face down fully clad including shoes and top-coats, handbags still over their arms and not a care in the world. No worries about where I was going to spend the next couple of nights. Not in Anne's cabin, still occupied by her two daughters, nor in any other cabin on a totally full ship. So where?

Well, if you're in show business you think show business! The disco! The answer lay in the booming multi-decibelled box that served as the late night dance spot. Surrounded by punters slightly less inebriated than my beloved and enjoying the alcoholic delights of a 'Gatsby' – Southern Comfort, lime juice, dry ginger and ice I spent man happy-ish hours. I learned all the words and actions to all the top songs of the day as I struggled to outstay all the hardened night-clubbers, waiting patiently for the last one to leave before stretching out on a bench seat to sleep.

Happy times, including the 4am awakening to the persistent poking of a drunken finger on to my chest and the beer-stained breath of a drunk who'd fallen asleep in the gents asking, 'Should there be two feet of water in the Carsey (great word for a loo) or is the ship sinking?'

How to answer those two questions? 'I'm not sure,' was all I could muster.'Thanks,' muttered the stranger as he lurched away and off into the night.In case he could have been right and the water might not be an overflow from the WC stalls, but something more serious, I moved position from bench to table-top and prayed that the water level would not rise too high as I slept.

Two nights later normality returned, dried out wine drinkers stopped feeling awful and promises never ever to imbibe on Madeira wine again had been sealed in blood. All was tranquil again on our cruise liner and surely that was all the disasters for one trip.

But no – not quite. Not for Johnny St Clair anyway. Johnny, a fine bass player and singer in a very talented trio had teamed up with us at meal times, a table being reserved especially for entertainers. I'm not sure if that was to keep the passengers away from us or vice versa. As events turned out it was probably the latter.

Our musical pal had been almost everywhere and seen almost everything. He was invaluable in terms of advice regarding travel, currency exchange and all shipboard procedures great and small.

His only apparent flaw would seem to have been his lack of patience with fools or wasters – not an ideal failing when dealing head on with the paying public. But then who'd have thought he'd ever get so head on?

Very much aboard ship, and extremely loud in all movements and opinions was a gentleman who wanted to be referred to as an 'internationalist' – always, to me, a cover up of a blurred early life in a country he no longer wished to represent – a bit like magicians calling themselves 'unusualists' in order to dissociate from the low-born rank and file trick doers.

Our international friend dressed predominantly in

white brocade and sported a suntan which owed much if not everything to a lamp in an upstairs room. He loudly boasted that he was en route to marry a Tongan princess in Monaco and had a Lagonda car in the hold of the ship to give her as a wedding present. Together they would travel the world and luxuriate in their combined wealth and bla-bla-bla-bla – ad nauseum.

It seemed to me that there was a cultural battle, if not war, about to break out when the 'internationalist came up against St Clair, the genuine man of the world – and so it proved.

Silly really, how it all began with 'She's a lassie from Lancashire,' Yes, looking back, silly is the word.

Our talented threesome were slowly but steadily breaking the ice in the ballroom - playing songs from near and far, requests and old time favourites - and had begun to whip up the various groups into some sort of sing-along world cup.

After Lancashire, and Yorkshire, and London we began to get more patriotic.For the Scots, 'I belong to Glasgow' - 'We'll keep a welcome' for the Welsh - 'Under the bridges of Paris' and even 'Midnight in Moscow' for the odd Russian. And it was about then that our 'internationalist' friend who had hidden his Berlin birthright came to the fore, strode up to the bandstand and bellowed at Johnny St Clair, 'You have played something for every country but you have done nothing German.'

'Okay Mate,' said our hero, 'Let's finish this number and then we'll invade Poland!'

Roars of laughter, weird German invective hurled and a stewards' enquiry by the Captain who could hardly keep a straight face whilst lecturing St Clair. As an aside, and nothing to do with the thread of this tale, I recently heard a similar story which tickled me.

A pal of mine, Mike Goddard, fine comedian and extremely talented writer, was nagged to entertain aboard a cruise liner working out of Miami. Having virtually an entirely American audience Mike tempered his humour to them and absolutely stormed the theatre on his first night.

Next day basking in the glory of his performance, having been congratulated by all and sundry, he was sunning himself on the upper deck when a lady approached and, pulling his foot in that waggly way that mothers have, said,

'Hey – we didn't like the way you mentioned Idaho last night.'

'Pardon?' muttered a startled Mike.

'Idaho. You mentioned Idaho in your act. We didn't like that.'

'I'm sorry, I don't recall saying Idaho,' said Goddard.

'In the joke about the postman! You mentioned Idaho!'

Quickly rattling through the postman gag, Mike said, 'But there are no bad references in the joke. It's just a simple story that requires a place name.'

'I know, but you shouldn't have picked on Idaho,' persisted the peroxide lady.'

Look madam, I could have used any name – Montreal, Washington, London. I just happened to drop on Idaho.'

'Yeah – well we didn't like that!' she droned.

'Please accept my apologies and let me assure you totally that I will never use Idaho again,' sighed a frustrated comic.

'Yeah – but you shouldn't have said Idaho in the first place!'

'That's done it,' steamed Mike as the final straw took affect. 'You have now said Idaho about six times. If you say it one more time, I swear I'll pick you up and throw you off this boat!!'

Off stormed Mrs Idaho and Mike sank back to enjoy the sun. But only for two minutes.

'Attention please! Attention please!' boomed the voice on the ship's tannoy.

'Mike Goddard to the Captain immediately. I repeat Mike Goddard to the Captain immediately!'

Off trudged Michael to face a captain whose furrowed brow told almost all the story.

'Mike, we have a problem,' he said gravely.

'I know Skipper, but the woman asked for it. She wouldn't shut up about Idaho and I ....'

The Skipper raised a hand to stop the outpourings

'Mike, just tell me this. Did you or did you not say that if she mentioned Idaho one more time you'd throw her off this boat?'

'Yes, Skip – I did.' Came the contrite reply.

'Mike,' said the furrowed browed one, 'This is not a boat – it's a ship!!! Never forget that!'

And the man was right. Ships are special. You can put a boat on a ship but you can't put a ship on a boat. Ships are special and I must return to my special adventures aboard Ithica.

After a three-day affair with Madeira wine and its after-effects the rest of our cruise was quite mundane - almost forgettable were it not for the sting in the tail.

A natural-born Scorpio, I should have been prepared but then life's better moments are the unexpected ones.

You will recall that I'd set off on my Odyssey bearing 1000 LP records to sell to the customers who would queue in their droves to buy two, three, or even four each? Well, reality proved those figures to be a little inflated.In fact, and in truth, the sum total sold to all aboard including one to the Skipper, was two!! Bad news, but worse to come! When subtracting two from a thousand it leaves an awful lot of vinyl to take home - and by air at that!

I'll never forget the scene at Manchester Airport as we lumbered through customs with two large suitcases (mostly my wife's luggage!) and a huge black trunk. Feeling half guilty, even with nothing to declare, we shuffled and skulked our way past a curious customs officer.

Having reached the safety of a five yard gap from him, and thinking all was now well, we began to visibly relax. That was the moment that we heard,

'Excuse me. What's in the trunk?'

Without turning around, I knew he was addressing me. Not knowing what to do in this case, I just paced backwards, dragging the wobbly baggage trolley in my reverse wake.

Never having been the confrontational type, I couldn't ask the questions that flashed through my mind, 'Why didn't you stop me in the first place? What was it that made my back more suspicious than my front?'

Instead, I just stood there mute and meek as the officer asked, 'What's in the box?'

(Sounds like a TV game show, doesn't it?')

'Records. LP records,' I spluttered.

'Are you a DJ or something?'

'No.' Can you believe it? Just 'No,' - what was I thinking of?

'Open it up, will you?'

'Yes' – just 'yes' I'd done it again!

As the trunk lid opened the officer stepped back as if he'd been hit with a smell of gas.

'These are all the same!' he hissed.

'I know.'

'They're all of you.'

That's right! 'Hmm,' he hummed. Then, scribbling furiously, with chalk on the trunk he sighed, 'Go on!'

'Thank you,' I said (I don't know why!) and proceeded towards the exit. Just as I reached it I received the final dart from Her Majesty's representative, 'Big head!'

I can still hear it echoing.............

Chapter 9

Ah - the ocean wave!

I think you'll agree that, having been through the fire myself, I'm allowed to relate events that have happened to other seafarers; those who travel the world in search of the exotic and unusual, little realizing that they are surrounded by both on board ship.

Take the old lady who approached a young bar steward on Canberra, the P&O Flagship.

'Excuse me young man, but can I ask you a serious question?'

'Fire away,' came the reply.

'Where do you go at night?'

'Pardon?' said the bemused seaman.

'Where do you go at night? I mean, you don't stay on the ship do you? There's no room.'

'No love,' said the sailor, 'The helicopter comes at one in the morning and takes us out to the oil rig.'

(Please bear in mind that this conversation is taking place in the middle of the Indian Ocean).

'To the oil rig? I thought as much,' purred the lady.

'Yes, and then it brings us back at five thirty in the morning ready for work.'

'Well, well, just as I'd imagined.'

Would you believe that the next day the passenger complained to the purser that the noise of the helicopter was keeping her awake? – TRUE.

Of course, once you've gathered a couple of comic stories such as the above, it's soon very easy to use them as a lure to glean other more outlandish tales from fellow passengers and, more particularly, crew.

A purser, from a shipping line which shall remain nameless, once regaled us with the events surrounding a world cruise and a very mild-mannered gentleman's plaintive request for help with 'him' – the other occupant of Cabin A58. It appears that events had been building up since departure from Southampton and had now reached unbearable pitch.

'You see,' explained our distressed one, 'It wouldn't be so bad if we had single beds.'

Apparently he was in one of the few cabins with a double bed and 'he' was abusing the facility.

'He won't take his socks off. Sleeps with them on and it's neither sanitary nor sweet-smelling.' (Great phrase!)

The purser enquired if our long-sufferer had complained to his bedmate about the strange habits.

'Not really,' he replied.

Surely though this had happened to him before ever they boarded the ship?

'Oh no – never!' came the startled response, 'I mean I'd never met the man before in my life!'

It seems the purser's office had cocked up a booking reference and, instead of a married couple, two complete strangers had been assigned A58. Cor blimey! Follow that if you can.

I think I can with the legendary tale of the Wolverhampton widow. Let's call her Betty in case she reads this book, although the events surely could only happen once, even at sea!

Betty spotted a bargain offer of a world cruise holiday in her local paper. The only string attached was that she would have to share a cabin with three other people. Obviously it would be easier if a group of friends or relatives went but, in Betty's case, she was alone and lonely and decided to risk being put in with three strangers.

Strangers the three were and, to make it more complicated, Swedish by nationality, having only a smattering of English between them. Nice people, though, and pleasant enough to talk to in sign language and garbled 'eurospeak'.

'Ja, isn't it? Yes,' Betty heard herself say at one point. Still, worse folk travel by sea, and our Wolverhampton wanderer seemed content that all would be well. However, language was not the only barrier that had to be crossed.

It seemed that all three Scandinavians loved the high life and the late nights in cabarets and discos, whilst our heroine loved early nights and crack of dawn mornings. Not to worry, though, because Betty had some mild sleeping tablets which would knock her out so soundly that she wouldn't hear the muffled noises of three drunken matrons attempting to disrobe in almost complete darkness.

And so it was that Betty crashed out at 9pm having pinned up her hair, oiled and waxed her face and neck and, finally, placed her false teeth in a bowl of Steradent-treated hot water placed on the dressing table. Sweet dreams and no disturbance. No sound, not even the odd alcohol-induced stumble, invaded her ears and 'Wolverhampton' enjoyed her most peaceful night in years. The liner gently pitching and rocking her and the thought of a great day at sea in the morning gently soothed her happy frame.

Too bad, indeed, that tomorrow had to come - the bright early dawn that only the sea brings. The feeling that all is well with the world, despite the deep-throated snoring of the Swedish synchronized sleeping team. Still, by the by, Betty was awake and all set to quietly dress and join the early risers for breakfast on the open deck.

Ah yes – breakfast at 7am. What could be better? Getting your teeth into a plate full of egg and bacon - this was the life! Teeth – ah yes, teeth. Now where were they? Of course, in the bowl. Which bowl? Why the one containing four pairs of false gnashers!

Yes, dear reader for our Swedes had returned, seen Betty's choppers and assumed it was an old British custom to share a denture bowl. God knows how many Betty tried before she found the right ones.

What did she do after that?

'I tied some coloured cotton around mine every night.' A bit like going to a party or wedding in the old days and all the knives and forks had bits of string on to tell whose were whose. And, while it's fine to smile at others misfortunes, it's easy to see how small predicaments can become enlarged out of all proportion when the sea is involved. Oh you vast oceans, you swelling seas and rivers, what havoc, both mental and physical, you can wreak with very little effort on your part.

Take one particular maiden voyage, no names no pack drill, that I was engaged on. Ostensibly it would be a straightforward crossing of the Bay of Biscay and a swift jaunt to the Canaries, Gibraltar, a little of the Med and then home. Easy.

The stuff of dreams you would think. So did I. Nothing easier than a leisurely shake-down cruise - short, sweet and not a high-risk venture. Oh yeah?? – Oh yeah?? I say again

Let's go from the top. Bay of Biscay – all things to all men (and women) – like a child really. When it's good it's very, very good. When it's bad forget it! Shake-down cruise, testing all working parts and putting things right whilst on the move. Fine perhaps in a brand new vessel, fresh from the shipyard and loaded with the latest advances in technology and comfort. Not quite the same as a veteran liner, brought from the Caribbean where her wide beam and flat bottom gently glided along the calm sundrenched waters, now hastily adapted for roughest weather. Too late discovered that she had a significant pitch and rolling motion when in any water which was even a smidge rougher than a millpond.

Add to the heady brew of mischief the fact that 60% of the crew were trainees; this would be their first serious trip and in some cases possibly their last, (I think they might have added if they lived that long)

Ah yes, all was set fair for disaster, although to look at the smiling faces and waving arms as we left Southampton to the strains of a military band, or was it a police band ......?

In retrospect it should have been a hospital ensemble but that fact was not obvious on day one, although day one was hardly over before the portents became ominous to all save the most naïve.

I will always recall that we hit the rough stuff at 10am on Christmas Eve morning and, at first, the vessel appeared to be coping. Stabilisers were heard to be put out and after a rocky minute and a half, appeared to have done the trick.

Then slowly, ever so slowly, we began to perceive the faintest of tremors and swings both up and down and side to side – an effect I've always referred to as 'the corkscrew' for obvious reasons. This constant inconstant movement brings out the worst in the poorer sailors and it wasn't long before the paper bags were being left dotted around the decks and stairwells for those whose tummies went first.

Wilder and wilder the jerkings and lurches became, and more and more fell under its spell. The great god of seasickness was gradually chewing up his more sensitive subjects.

On and on ploughed the ship, itself impervious to the motion, but lord what an upset it was causing its children. Staff, raw and never used to high seas, began to join the missing list as trays of drinks or pots of tea were unceremoniously dropped (literally) and the carriers hastened to the dubious safety of the nearest loo!

A queasy sort of panic settled on the passengers and they even began to admit they were ill (totally un-British) and began to ask for advice.

'Get a large port and brandy down you. It's called a stabilizer,' I offered.

'No good – the bar staff have disappeared.'

'Alka Seltzer?' I suggested.

'The shop's just shut. He's as sick as a dog.'

'The doctor. Go to see the doctor on D-deck,' I suggested. (Desperate moments now these.)

'Never make it mate! Never make it!' came the reply, mumbled through the fingers of the hand across his mouth that was vainly trying to keep his breakfast down.

'Then get as low on the ship as you can so that the rocking from side to side is not as pronounced.' I shouted at his back as it disappeared. 'Pronounced?' – hell of a word to use in the midst of a storm at sea.

'Ah well,' I mused, 'I've done all that can be done; may as well relax and enjoy the solitude of the grand lounge – just me and the piano-tuner. 'Hell of a time to be doing that', I thought, but never said.

The day never got any better but I suddenly developed a problem – no, not of the seasickness kind but a bit more physical.

Before sailing I did what all good travellers should do – had a haircut ashore. I never trust scissors-wielders on the waves. Too many bumps and chances of a 'mis-snip'.

I'd been to Ray, my normal barber; full of chat and wise advice he is, but always delivered to the back of your head and the mirror –(one day I must check what colour eyes he has!)

'Everton aren't doing so well,' he suggested, picking on my weak spot.

'No?'

'Terrible last week,' he affirmed.

'Really?'

'I'll tell you how bad we were. We wouldn't have scored of we'd had a ball each!'

'Your hair's in good nick,' he chirped, getting back to my strong spot. 'But if you're away for a while I'd better take it down a little.'

This was usually the clarion call for a crew cut but I made him promise to go steady. And, fair play, he did. But, of course, as with all hairdressers' snippings, a lot of stray bits are left behind after the final comb-through and consequently brush off the collar. So many stray bits in fact that it often takes two washings or showers to remove all traces.

The reason I am boring you with such details will soon become evident as I return you to the deepest, roughest seas of the North Atlantic and a shipload of seasick souls.

In the course of my wanderings around the decks, both inner and outer, sympathizing, advising, directing, admonishing all those less fortunate than myself it was suddenly that the side effects of Ray's snipping became apparent. For some reason a tiny piece of grey hair had found its way into my eye and, try as I might, I could neither see it nor remove it. Lifting one lid over the other, eyewashes – nothing worked.

'Medical Centre,' insisted the good Yorkshire lady, 'Mrs O'.

'Yes dear,' I mumbled meekly and set off to D-deck and the ship's doctor.

D-deck is long and usually deserted except for the odd cabin steward trundling buggies full of linen and washing liquid. But not today! Today was special, like rush hour in London, or the M25 when a horse gets loose and gallops up and down – nose to tail of concerned faces, none happy, all strained and pained.

I'd hit the back of the queue for treatment. Each person, European, Asian and African had all managed to become the same colour – grey! All sat resignedly waiting to see the doctor or die, whichever came the sooner.

I began to fear that I would never be treated this side of Gibraltar when a firm voice from the other end – roughly 300 yards – bellowed, 'Are you ill?'

'No, doctor,' I shouted back.

'Then come to the front!'

What a weird exchange of words, making little or no

sense to me or 'le Miserables' around me.

Apparently there was a delay whilst the nurse replenished the stocks of vaccine and the doc could concentrate on normal matters. What a doctor, and what a place to be a doctor. In the course of 24 hours he treated 800 sea-sick passengers and 300 crew. At £40 per passenger it would appear that his earnings are far in excess of Elton John or Madonna, without singing a note!

Still – anyone who works at sea in the service of the public deserves all they are paid. Without wishing to be cruel, or even picky, the public afloat are the worst, but also funniest, people to deal with.

'Nowt as queer as folk,' is a good description, but it only goes part of the way.

Take the lady who asked for, and received, a single berth cabin aboard a luxury cruise liner. Her first trip and, by sheer misfortune, her cabin steward's first ever day at sea. How fate can contrive to pick such a combination no-one will ever know.

Bright as a button, Madame X boarded and, in a flurry of tickets, handbags and well-wishes from relatives, entered her cabin, shared a few chosen words with Steward Sam, and then closed her cabin door to lie down and rest.

Sam decided that it would not be gentlemanly to disturb a lady's slumbers and vowed to wait until he was beckoned before going back to her cabin.

And so it was that Madame was reported missing when she didn't appear for lunch, lifeboat drill, evening meal or breakfast. A search party, headed by the deputy purser (always more efficient than the real thing!) was mustered and quickly zoned in on the cabin steward.

'I haven't seen her since yesterday when she went to lie down,' he muttered.

A medium-weight pounding on the door was answered by an underweight call of, 'Come in'.

The entire posse entered the cabin to find Lady X seated on the end of her bunk obviously distraught.

'I thought you'd never come,' she spluttered.

'But why didn't you just open the door?' they asked.

'I opened it but it's just a bathroom.'

'Yes, but why didn't you open this main door,' they pressed.

'Well, it had a card with 'do not disturb' hanging on the door knob and I didn't want to intrude!' True story!

And if you think that's odd .... what about the stowaway?

Oh yes – there have been many in history. There'll probably be many more to come. I only ever met one and that was by a complete fluke.

It's a well-known fact that you must never underestimate the power of little old ladies. Funny they may be – even a little odd sometimes – but a force to be reckoned with. Whenever I hear a little old lady story I always think of my mother and how she'd have reacted.

Take the two dears at a bus stop when a flash car pulled up, driver's window went down and Mr Cool behind the wheel asked, 'Parlez vous Francais?'

'No dear,' came the answer.

'Sprechen sie Deutsch?'

'Sorry.'

'Parliarmo Italiano?'

'Can't help you, love.'

As an exasperated motorist screeched off, one said to the other, 'Mary, you know we are ignorant. We should have learned a second language.'

'I wouldn't bother,' reasoned Mary. 'He knows three and it's done him no good!'

Ah yes – little old lady reasoning! Hard to beat at any time. And particularly when sailing the oceans with time to relax and ponder.

Well do I recall the first leg of a world cruise on that beautiful P&O ship Canberra – sadly now gone for razor blades. It was about four days out of home port when a brace of LOLs (got the abbreviation?) approached the purser and said, 'We've a complaint about a male passenger. We think something should be done about him.'

What could this be – molestation? – drunken hijinks? – bad language? No, no. Simpler than that (well, nearly!).

'He never buys us a drink. Never. And it's not right.'

'Well, well, an original complaint,' thought the purser. 'This'll go down in the annals for certain. I must ensure that my name is linked with it.'

But back to the complaint. Simple in real terms. Each passenger is given a credit card-type pass which is used for boarding and disembarking as a form of recognition. Also it can be used to purchase goods that are later charged to the cabin account and guaranteed by a swipe of a credit card. The little piece of plastic can even help trace your whereabouts aboard ship. How did we ever live without it? Of course, as with all things modern, there is a downside and so we move to our unfortunate gentleman on Canberra.

It appears that every day he would meet the same two ladies for the ballroom dancing class and they would enjoy a chat and when the waiter came around they'd have a wee sherry or a glass of wine together. But at no time did Sir Galahad even offer to pay never mind actually cough up.

Now I think you or I would have been quite happy

to shun the fellow's company after a couple of days but not these old girls. They wanted justice and so they approached the purser. It wasn't long before the whole truth became evident.

The man was a stowaway, sleeping in a lifeboat at night, rising early and having a huge buffet breakfast on deck – no need for table reservations. Then he'd spend the morning joining all the shipboard events, feast on a deck buffet lunch and filling a doggy-bag for later that evening.

So – with no worries, he intended to see the world free of charge – providing he stayed on board, and providing he kept away from the two 'Miss Marples'!

When the jig was up the purser told our little gadfly that he would be put ashore at the next port of call and returned to Blighty.

'Aagh. Do me a favour mate,' he pleaded. 'Let me stay on till Miami.'

'OK,' beamed purser Pete, 'On one condition.'

'Anything.'

'You tell us how you got on board the ship in the first place.'

'Easy mate,' said Stowaway Sam.

'In Southampton I arrived with a wooden crate containing my luggage, a large oily spanner and dressed in greasy overalls. I just put the crate on my shoulder and carried it up the gangplank following other crewmen.'

This lending credence to the fact that, where the British are concerned, if you keep moving and look as if you know what you're doing, nobody stops or questions you.

So far we've looked at odd tales at sea. But what about when the cruisers disembark to savour the delights of foreign ports and foreign parts? What happens to the poor unsuspecting ones? – no, not the passengers, the local inhabitants!!

Little do those poor foreigners realize what lies in store for them as up to three thousand lobster red, flip-flop wearing, plastic bag carrying emissaries of the great White Queen descend upon their shores, trying valiantly to blend in with the locals and looking for exotic beauty spots, excellent cuisine and spectacular bargains – all in three and a half hours and for less than £10.

Believe me, no matter how travelled we become, how worldly wise and, yes, even conceited, the pitfalls are still there for all to see – well, at least in hindsight.

Take me, a right clever dick on the topic of world travel and countries visited. I'm not saying I know it all, or have been everywhere, but it's a close run thing. Why I've got such confidence in my own abilities, or at least I had, that it would be hard to throw me. Why - aren't I the one who commissioned a special T-shirt when I first went to America. Oh, yes, what fun I had shopping in stores and restaurants and letting the checkout girl or waitress glimpse those magic words emblazoned on my chest, 'Don't tell me what sort of a day to have!'

Oh boy! How that ruined their parting words leaving them tongue-tied and dumbfounded.

How funny – how utterly hilarious! Yes, I'm the guy (sorry was the guy) without a care. I say was because, just like my T-shirt, it doesn't take much to bring a person down to earth – particularly people like me, the arrogant type.

Look at the first leg of our world cruise on Canberra. Southampton to San Francisco – Winter to Summer – in about fourteen days of steady steaming.

Ideal, thought I, to nurture a suntan of impressive

proportions, having the time and conditions to turn a gradual golden brown like the multi-seasoned regulars on the travel circuit. OK – so we had to cross the Bay of Biscay and the unpredictable Atlantic Ocean, but who cares as long as all passengers started at roughly the same colour and if I missed not one minute of sunshine then, theoretically, I would receive as much of a tanning as the rest. Unfortunately I received a tanning of the pride that I'd never forget.

Having spent every waking and almost every sleeping hour in the open air, and having applied various sun blocks of various strengths to all parts of my exposed carcass, I was fit and ready when our ship reached sunny Jamaica. How proud I felt striding down the gangplank, ready to achieve my lifetime's ambition of 'blending in' with the folk of the West Indies.

The illusion lasted about twenty seconds. Adjacent to the ship and stretched along the quay, were rows and rows of stalls selling the local produce – mangoes, watermelons and such. And it was from one of these emporiums that the lady's voice rang out, 'Hey, Mister Pinkman, Mister Pinkman!' and do you know, even with my back turned I could tell she meant me! Oh suntan, oh suntan – how you flattered to deceive!

Of course I blame the lure of the sea for lots of life's calamities. It's the sea, and all its weird and wonderful properties, which affects the brains of we humble mortals and makes us do things we wouldn't dream of doing on dry land. I mean, look at Miss New Zealand.

Miss New Zealand was not a young person, nor was she small. About 85 years and 200 lbs, but brimming with health and life and vitality. Well, she was a lass who'd been everywhere and back again, enjoyed all of life's experiences and was now in 'middle age' (her words) feeling as if it was all passing her by. Not quite desperate yet, she was still prone to bemoaning her fate to any passing male, married or no.

'Every woman on this ship has a man except for me. Do you think that's fair?' she would ask whilst keeping you pinned against a wall. 'Am I not attractive?' she'd demand of weak and strong alike.

'Er .. of course,' would splutter the unwitting one.

'Then why don't you come to my cabin? I've got plenty of booze.'

One day I had the temerity to ask, 'Have you no Smarties?'

'Smarties?' she bellowed, 'Smarties? What are they? I'll get some if you'll come to my cabin.'

I scarpered, and so did every available and unavailable man on board, leaving her desperate. How desperate we didn't realize until we docked in Fiji.

A beautiful country, warm climate, warm-hearted people and an ideal spot from which to bring home souvenirs, although what is a souvenir to one person may not be to another.

I mean, how can you class a roll of lino as a 'memento of my visit' which is what our Amazonian, middleager claimed. She almost got away with it, and would have done had it not been for the eagle eye of Barney Martin the officer in charge on deck when two brawny Fijians tried to manhandle the lino up the gangplank.

Sadly for Miss New Zealand, Barney had once worked for a removal firm and could make a fairly good 'guesstimate' of items and their weight. Yes, he was a man who could tell when something looked heavier than it should.

'Put it down boys,' he barked, still numb at the idea that anyone would travel halfway around the world to bring home a roll of floor-covering.

'Let's have a shufti,' he ordered, and began unrolling the oil-cloth to reveal a live and lusty 16 year old Fijian lad who'd been 'bewitched' by the lady from Auckland.

'I've got booze in my cabin,' was not apparently the phrase she'd used on this young fellow. It seems that money and free passage was more of a lure. Either way, it didn't work and she was doomed to sail the seven seas forever manless, boyless and increasingly desperate.

Cruising, like that though – it has highs. It has lows. And in the end you lower your sights and settle for whatever turns you on. To this extent I tend to believe sea stories – even the most farfetched.

Like the super-duper bargain world cruise epic. Never heard about it? Well, supposedly it went like this ......

A person, friend or relative of the narrator, spotted an ad in a Sunday supplement saying, 'World cruise, all found, £28.' Fearing the price was possibly short of two noughts at the end, our hero phoned in and was assured that the total of £28 was indeed correct and would he like to book. Yes – he blooming well would! And yes he did!

Six weeks later he received his sailing details, being bidden to arrive in Southampton at Dock Gate X at a specific time to be taken aboard. On arrival he was greeted by a rather dubious looking character clad in blue and white hooped sweatshirt, torn denims and plimsolls. He was only short of an eye-patch to look like a pirate.

'You for the world cruise mate?' he muttered.

'Er, yes, that's me!'

'Well, you realize that because of the low price there are one or two things not quite up to first class standard.'

'Oh, yes of course.'

'First one is, we don't have a launch to take you to the ship. In fact you have to make your own way in this .... ,' he said, pointing to towards the world's most decrepit rowing boat, covered in barnacles and rust and almost awash with sludgy water.

'Hey-ho,' thought our bargain hunter, 'a small price to pay for such a cheap cruise.'

Having reached the main vessel – very sleek and shipshape looking and bearing the name 'TRIRENE' he clambered aboard to be met by a surly, shady-looking oik who said, 'You here on the £28 deal?'

'Erm, yes.'

'Follow me,' he growled, 'And put these on.' And suddenly our world traveller was handcuffed and being led below.

'Trirene, Trirene,' as he stumbled down the stairways the name began to race around his puddle head.

'Trirene,' – yes that was it, an ancient galley-ship with three decks of oars – oars?? – Oars?? Don't tell me – oh but yes!

As recognition dawned and as the penny was dropping and not quite hitting the floor he realized he was about to be fettered to a long galley oar, joining three other people. Looking behind and ahead he could make out more and more unfortunates like himself, chained and padlocked in. Probably as many as a hundred and twenty cut-price travellers were on his deck, so multiplied by three, the Trirene had at least 360 potential rowers. In real terms, a huge saving on fuel oil.

As his eyes finally adjusted to the light, it became apparent that at the front of the ship was a huge drum and behind it stood a man of seven feet and twenty-odd stones who suddenly began to pound out a rhythm on the drum.

Other men of similar proportions paced up and down the lines of oars using bullwhips to beat the chained up travellers into a steady rowing motion.

'My God!' shrieked our hero, 'I can't believe this. 'What a way to treat passengers in this day and age. I'm going to write to my MP when I get home. Can you believe the whips and chains? And what about the bloke on the big drum?'

I know,' said the raver next to him.

'He's not as good as the one we had last year!!'

Chapter 10

The Brit abroad

Being an island race, we British have a heritage that is bound firmly with the sea and so it usually comes as no surprise when odd things happen or are reported to have happened. Now and again we see for ourselves. And so it is with me. I haven't been everywhere, nor seen everything, but you might appreciate a few of my experiences.

Like the time aboard Sea Princess (now renaimed Victoria) – a fine ship carrying about seven hundred passengers – large enough to ride out stormy seas, small enough to have that 'cosy' personal feeling and with cabins of a size to suit even the most extravagantly-minded folk. She was on a world cruise and we joined her in Japan en route to the Suez Canal, the Med and then home.

One port we'd been looking forward to exploring was Singapore – legend having it that here would be the source of good quality, good value electronics and clothing. 'Change Alley' had been recommended as the place to purchase music tapes, discs and players and to seek out the finest and quickest tailors and dressmakers.

So it was with a feeling of anticipation and elation that we crowded the top deck to watch our entry and docking in the harbour. We couldn't wait but had to wait – a jolly sight longer than we'd expected or than anyone else had had to wait. An hour of chugging slowly, hardly moving, chugging again, appearing to stop altogether, and even appearing to go in reverse! Why? Why? Soon it became evident through the grapevine that the trouble lay not with us, but with others. An Italian freighter to be exact. A freighter which refused to leave our berth because she was three short of a full crew.

'But,' reasoned our captain in discussions with port officials, 'If my ship were three people short I would still sail!'

'Not,' replied the port authorities, 'If the three were the Captain and his wife and the first mate!'

Apparently the second mate didn't fancy the task or the risk and so we stewed for three hours!

But not all sea adventures end in frustration. Sometimes they end in glory and a deep inward feeling of satisfaction as you say to yourself, 'I was there – I'll always be able to relate the story.'

My memorable occasion involved a leg of the world cruise aboard the P&O ship, Sea Princess. We were crossing the Indian Ocean en route to Australia when we received a distress call from a ship called Ocean Pearl. She was on fire and, as far as we know, adrift and wide open to the elements.

Her captain's biggest worry was that the watertight doors would not hold for very much longer and that the fire, already intense, would spread and cause the huge funnel to collapse downwards through the ship and take the whole vessel with it. Her passengers, mostly Americans of mature years, had mustered bravely on deck with their bags and had sat calmly throughout what must have been a traumatic night awaiting rescue.

Of all the vessels in close proximity we were the nearest and the fastest and we arrived early morning and our crew set about the rescue procedure. At this point it's time I asked you, dear reader, a personal question. Have you ever seen events unfold and thought how proud you were – a) to be a part of the proceedings, if only in a minor role - and b) to belong to the same nationality as the main players? You know that wonderful feeling that says,

'These are our boys and girls performing this amazing feat?' And the feat was truly amazing.

Steadily, with no signs of panic or overdue haste, our little motor launches set off toward Ocean Pearl and, as calm as you like, began to pick up the Americans, luggage and all, and chug them safely back to Sea Princess.

In a little, unending, circular stream they offloaded each and every one of those brave, long-suffering passengers and brought them to the safety and well-organised bosom of our ship where the pursers had already re-jigged the accommodation to fit in an extra 300 or so folks.

British people were happily agreeing to 'double up' to make room for the 'rescued perishing' and the caterers were fast reaching the point of increasing production of breakfasts to feed the tired and hungry newcomers.

Of course, in the heat of all this effort and heroism, there had to be the odd quirky story or two. My favourite, involving our own British folk, was the pair of old dears, staring over the side at the 'rescuers' clambering up rope netting and commenting, 'Isn't it perfectly disgraceful that first-class passengers have to board in this way?' Sorry ladies, but, had the roles been reversed, I think you'd have been delighted to board that way – or upside down or sideways for that matter. Regarding our friends from the US, let me give you a cor-blimey anecdote. It involved a lady of considerable means who was lucky enough to be billeted in a suite of rooms along with her British equivalent who had kindly offered accommodation. She was aboard only minutes before striding down to the purser's office and demanding that the suite owner be ousted out as, 'I've never had to share a room with anyone, and I'm not starting now!'

However, on being offered the alternative of a return trip to the burning Ocean Pearl, our lady quite quickly decided to see things in a reasonable light. Ah life – how increasingly strange are your workings!

'Of all the bars in all the world' was a legendary Humphrey Bogart quote from 'Casablanca' but 'of all the memorials in all the world' is mine and mine alone.

My life's ambition had always been to visit and pay homage to the shrine of USS Arizona at Pearl Harbour. So – when the opportunity arose to work on a cruise ship which called at Hawaii, there was no holding me back. And so it came to pass, and a long-time wish to stand where millions had preceded me, and honour the fallen was realized.

But realization has many forms and as I stood, head bowed, amongst the throng from all over the world (including Japan) I was approached by one of the Hawaiian guides.

'Excuse me, but I think I know you,' he said. 'Would you be Tom O'Connor?'

'Yes, I would,' I replied but how would a guide in

Hawaii know me – a retired schoolteacher from Liverpool?

'Well,' he explained, 'I was on a course in England last year and I caught the 'flu and was in bed for ten days and watched your show *Crosswits* every day.'

'Was I proud as Punch at the news? And was I double proud to receive the adulation of other holidaymakers when they realized I might be a person of note. To be honest, my greatest moment was when a party of Japanese thought I was a famous golfer and asked for my autograph. I proceeded to scribble a totally indecipherable name which could have been Montgomerie, Tiger Woods or Olazabel – and they seemed happy enough. Proof if proof were needed that some people are easily pleased – whilst others certainly aren't.

I'm talking about 'picky' people. Do you know what I mean? Those good folk who can find fault in almost anything. Like the super 'Mr Picky' who died and went to Heaven and St Peter said, 'Come in – but you won't like it!'

Now I've got a friend like that – a fine fellow – a hero in sport and a super hero in adversity. I refer to the motorcycling legend Eddie Kidd who, before the tragic spill that wrecked his career and his body, was probably one of the most famous faces on Earth. And what a handsome face, one that hid the fact that the man behind was quite a picky eater – picky to say the least. Not the world's easiest to cater for – and that's praising him!

And it happened, as things tend to do, that the great man went on a trip to Thailand to soak up the rays and rest from the bumping and bouncing of stunt-biking – an exhilarating sport to watch, and a sport requiring no driving licence because, believe it or not, Eddie has never passed a driving test in his life!

Whilst taking his ease in a quiet little village he was approached by the local police chief who had heard on the grapevine that Eddie was famous and, more importantly, obliging. Would the great man give the village a demonstration of his skills? Sure he would – and sure he did (as the Irish would say).

After a burn-up and a succession of wheelies and other stunts, the great Mr Kidd was honoured with a huge feast with tables laden with food and drink, and music till dawn. But what to eat? What was what?

'This is rattlesnake meat.'

'No thanks,' muttered Eddie, tight-lipped.

'What about fried octopus?'

'Certainly not! You'll have me heaving.'

'Well, what do you eat?' asked an exasperated chef.

'Bacon sandwiches,' came the resolute British reply.

'Bacon off a pig?'

'That's it,' said our hero.

'Easy,' said the gourmet reaching for a huge knife and slicing a piece of the backside of a hapless pig that was passing by. Amid squeals and outpourings of blood, the cook threw the slice of raw meat into a frying pan and reached for some bread.

'Oh God,' said Eddie, 'That's disgusting. I couldn't possibly eat that – yuk!'

'No?' said the chef. 'Never mind,' and threw the fried bacon on the ground whereupon the pig ate it!

How Mother Nature can recycle things is a wonder beyond compare – or as my pal Eddie often quotes, 'What a world, when you've got pigs eating their own bums!'

Chapter 11

It's the people!

There used to be a song, years ago, called 'There's no place like home for the holidays' and to this day many people would say it was true. 'Home' gives the impression of comfort and safety amongst your nearest and dearest. Well, dearest would still apply in lots of cases and, 'nearest' may relate to the distance travelled, but may not encompass all that is best in travel or arrival.

Years ago it was the norm to travel to the British seaside and stay in a guest house or small hotel for a couple of weeks, regardless of the weather or whatever the fates might have in store.

One natural hazard in those days would be the seaside landlady who awaited you in her domain when you arrived tired and hungry from a coach or train journey that could have taken many hours more than it should. Most of these lovely lasses were of the kind and obliging sort – but not all. Hence conversatons like, 'My bed feels very damp. I'll have lumbago in the morning.'

'You certainly won't. You'll have cornflakes like everyone else!'

Or the legendary guest house tale of the landlady carving up the Saturday chicken, 'Where are you from?' she asked of one.

'Hull,' came the reply – and she proceeded to give him the right wing.

'And you -?' she asked of the second.

'Liverpool,' said he and was rewarded with the left wing.

'Where are you from?' she said to the third.

'Southend, but I'm not hungry!' came the reply.

Ah – happy days! Days of carefree fun – great to look back on from a distance – and the further the better say we all.

Take Max Boyce, fine fellow, a comic legend and a superb observer of everyday humour. He manages to see and relate the funny side of everyday life, none funnier than his own experiences. If you ever meet him, ask him to tell you about his trip to the Norfolk Broads!

It seems that the young Boyce and a gang of ne'er-do-wells had travelled from their native Wales to the beautiful countryside of East Anglia and had decided to relax in the time-honoured way of those parts by renting a narrow boat to live on and navigate through the Broads and their many locks - and to call at the various hostelries along the way.

All went well with their not-too-ambitious plans until, after two or three days of shunting up and down, they had a mutual rush of blood and went for the big one – a trip to Great Yarmouth – a twofold mission! One, to prove it could be done and two, to watch the Summer show featuring Freddy Starr.

As connoisseurs of comedy will know, Freddy is a very funny man but even he would be hard pushed to find something to rival the Welshmens' exploits.

The story goes that our intrepid 'narrow-boaters' steered their way successfully to Great Yarmouth, calling at all pubs west and found a handy space to moor up. Off they went to the show, little knowing the finer points of seamanship. Little details, you know, like the fact that Yarmouth has the second fastest water level fall in Europe! So when they eventually returned to their vessel full of fun, booze and curry they became aware of a creaking noise rending the air.

'More of a tortured screech than a creak,' Max assured me.

It certainly attracted a large crowd, not only standing and gaping but, in a lot of cases mumbling, muttering and even laughing out loud. What could it be? What act of lunacy could demand so much attention? What sort of idiot was abroad on the Broads?

Well, it was the Welsh sort of idiot. The sort that ties up a narrow boat, forgets about the tide fall and returns to find the vessel swinging in mid-air – hanging by the two mooring ropes and creaking to and fro.

Swiftly the boys realized that a hasty retreat from the scene was in order. Get out of the way and wait for high tide. This they did and, under cover of darkness, they tried to undo the huge knots in the ropes, but to no avail. The weight of the boat had pulled the knots too tight to be released so the only answer was to cut them away with an axe – thus attracting further crowds. And so it came to pass that the Welsh wizard got his first taste of public laughter and notoriety, albeit of the worst kind - laughing at instead of laughing with. But none-the-less a memorable moment!

I always think it's nice to have the odd story to tell at dinner parties but some stories can be odder than others.

Often the events appear unbelievable at the time and

even more incredible when time and retelling have left their embellishments. For sure any story involving an elephant has got to be in the top drawer for interest. Whether the tale is the stuff of legend or just prefabrication it always brings a smile when told, of the day a hapless gent and his family decided to visit their local safari park.

Having sweated in an air condition-free, overheating car whilst the interminable queue crawled towards and through the much undermanned (aren't they always?) toll booths, they eventually broke clear into the park itself and gaily trolled along, enthusing over the wonders of nature and decrying mankind for the years of cruelty inflicted upon animals throughout history.

They even got to remarking that one would have to be a heartless beast of a person even to merely dislike one of God's creatures. This led them to consider writing to the safari park hierarchy and loudly praising their efforts in returning these beautiful creatures to their own safe habitat, albeit in shores far from their historical roots.

Ah yes. All this and more would surely have led to the formation of an action group and other noble ventures, if it hadn't been for the elephant. Just the one! Mind you, one is all it takes to ruin your day when it sits on the bonnet of your car!

Apparently this is what happened to our animal loving friends and not only did it put a huge dent in the metal, in fact bending it into the contours of the engine underneath, but it also completely incapacitated the vehicle. This led the family to loudly proclaim references to the animal kingdom that two minutes ago would have seemed impossible to believe. References to the 'idiots' who ran the safari park and their total lack of thought for the poor unprotected humans who were totally at the mercy of these savage beasts which should all be caged up out of harm's way. Ah – how just one elephant can make a difference!

Mind you, man's inhumanity to animals and vice versa, is as nothing compared with man's thoughtlessness towards his fellow man – particularly the hard-pressed, down-trodden motorist. They used to say, 'only in America', but that adage has now become more worldwide and particularly so in Ireland.

The Emerald isle – home of the leprechaun and the banshee! The country which does not recognize the word manana – because 'we have nothing so immediate.' Aha yes, Erin. The land of comeday-goday – where the impossible is always possible and the unbelievable is everyday.

If all this appears to be hard to comprehend I'll call my first witness – Jim McCall. A citizen of Dublin town, hard-bitten in the world of hi-tech business, experienced in the ways of the world. A hard man to convince, an all-round tough cookie – well until the night he lost his car.

Hey, not just any car, but a brand new, top of the range, Lotus Europa – gleaming white, pristine in all respects and the all time McCall dream. So proud was he that, on the day of purchase, he had already worked out his route from Dublin to Mullingar to perform his first test run. This road is now as modern as most today but at the time of the Lotus trip it left a lot to be desired. The old rule applied that 'just because there's grass in the middle, it doesn't mean it's a dual carriageway.'

So on a lazy summer's evening Jim drove out to the heartland and, having performed all the twists and turns required to assess the road holding, resolved to make for home at as fast a speed as he could muster as the darkness closed in.

Averaging, he guessed, around 70 mph, he was cornering like a Formula One driver and opening up to over 100 mph on what straights there were. Unfortunately it was on a shortish straight, as the night darkened, that he saw the aeroplane. No, not above high and flying level, but just in front of him, about three hundred yards, and descending upon him at great speed.Hitting the brakess and changing gears down, McCall attempted to spin off the road away from the oncoming plane. To no avail! The speed, the braking, the wheels locked in a vain attempt to swerve - all served to prevent control of the car and she rolled over three or four times, virtually writing it off and leaving Jim, badly bruised and shaken, but alive at least.

But what about the aircraft? Did it land? Did the pilot pull back the throttle and claw for height? No. It just went breezing by on its way to the West. You see, plane there was none. No. Merely a lorry transporting cars from Dublin's docks to Sligo on a dark night. Baffled? Well, it was like this. For some reason the lights on the truck failed and, left in the dark both literally and metaphorically, the driver had hit on the blinding idea to switch on the lights of the top car on the transporter, thus allowing their beam to angle down at 45 degrees and brighten his road ahead. The road was certainly brighter than he was, as he totally ignored the affect the downward beams would have on the mind of an oncoming motorist.

Boy, what an insurance tangle that must have been to unravel!

And here's another, just as complicated, but at least a little more humorous; not that I believe the story has any basis at all. Never in a month of Sundays. Never ever. Not even in the land of the almost legendary feats of showbusiness and entertainment.

Blackpool! Fairest city of all when talking about summer vacations throughout history. The 'Wakes Weeks' which saw thousands, probably millions, of folk from factory, farm and coalmine, shipyard, dockyard and office. The people of the North taking their ease on the Golden Mile, the piers, the souvenir shops, the funfairs, the chip shops, cafes, ice cream and candy floss parlours.

A 'season' which, at its height, ran from middle-May to late October, culminating in 'the lights' – Blackpool's world-renowned illuminations which were, and still are, an electrical and neon miracle which runs all along the promenade up and over Blackpool Tower and almost out to Morecambe.

It was, supposedly, some years ago when a middle-aged gent knocked on the door of a typical guest house and requested accommodation.

'Certainly dear,' smiled the landlady, 'Fifty pounds a week, B&B.'

'But I like funny breakfasts,' said the holidaymaker.

'No problem,' he was assured, '£50 is all in with full use of cruet!'

'But I like beans, I mean a lot of beans, for breakfast,' he added.

'No problem dear, honestly,' came the smiling reply.

So morning one, our guest proceeded to eat four large platefuls of beans on toast and, happy as you please, nodded to the landlady and strode off towards the town centre. Two hours later two police officers arrived brandishing a picture of the holidaymaker.

'Have you seen this man?' they asked.

'Yes, he's staying here.'

'Well, we've some bad news for you. We've just found his body at the foot of Blackpool Tower. We think he may have thrown himself off!' one muttered grimly.

'I can't believe that,' she replied in all innocence, 'Because he was full of beans when he left here!!'

OK, OK – maybe the story isn't true. What do you mean it definitely isn't??

But if you think that tale is ludicrous, why don't we finish this chapter with a real humdinger? Here's a story passed on to me by the first national journalist I ever met. A fine fellow called Jim who worked in the Northern office of the Daily Mirror. Long gone to the great printing presses in the sky now, I'll always remember and thank Jim for one of the most classic 'true happenings' that ever graced my act.

Based, as I was, in Liverpool in the early days it suited me to base my observational comedy on docks, dockers and the sea, and any sea yarn has always half a chance of being believed or at worst, acknowledged as possible if not probable. So here goes! Picture the scene .... a Liverpool dockside pub on Christmas Eve evening. The bars are laden with not so sober revellers, singing, swaying, feeling happy, feeling queasy but all attempting to rise to the festive season. All that is, except one lady in her fifties and in her cups. No laughter here, no music, just sadness and a single tear threatening to fall from the eye above the burning half inch of cigarette dangling from her quivering lip.

'I can't believe you,' she sobbed to her husband who was busy destroying 'Danny Boy'. 'How can you be so happy when our Billy's all on his own at Christmas?'

'Whaa??' came the disinterested reply.

'Our Billy, on his own. Someone should be with him tonight,' she went on.

'Whaa??' Our Billy? He's in America. He's in New York. How can anyone be with him? After all he was the one who went away .... 'the pipes, the pipes are calling!'

'Yeah, but he shouldn't be on his own,' persisted mother, shuffling her slippered feet.

'But it's ten o'clock, there's no planes, no ships, there's not even any buses,'spluttered dad. 'It's impossible.'

'I won't sleep tonight, worrying. I know I wont.'

'All right,' bellowed 'Danny Boy' 'All right. That's settled it. I'm going to New York – Now!'

'How?' asked his mates at the bar.

'I'm going to row! That's how,' he bellowed and made his way out of the pub and off toward the harbour wall, followed by the entire pub. As fate would have it there was a small rowing boat moored on a capstan and Charlie leapt aboard. Provisions in the guise of two crates of Guinness and fifty cigarettes were thrown aboard and the crowd cheered as he grabbed the oars and struck out for the new world. Back the revellers went to the pub which stayed open all night as a farewell to Charlie gesture. But at about eleven thirty one bar fly said to another,

'What did you do with the mooring rope of Charlie's boat?'

'Me? Nothing. I thought you had it.'

'No,' said the first,' I never untied it.'

'Neither did I,' said the other.

'Blimey,' said the first as the light dawned.

'He's still tied up to the quay!!'

Down ran the pair to the harbour wall where they could hear the splash of oars in the pitch darkness.

'Charlie,' they called in unison. 'Charlieeee!!'

'Bloddy hell,' came the voice from the boat,' That's incredible. No-one knows me in New York!'

Thanks for that, Jim.

Chapter 12

Taxi!!

Are you the same as I am? When you think of travel are your first thoughts of planes, ships and trains? Isn't it peculiar that we always tend to go for transport that is the furthest from our reach? Hardly ever in our minds is the more frequently used, and often wrongly reviled, taxi cab.

Many a Saturday night has been saved by that reliable old warhorse the Black Cab, Mini Cab or licensed Hackney MPV. Many a courtship has been assisted by the arrival of 'the cavalry' long after the last bus home has gone.

Many a business meeting threatened by traffic congestion has been saved at the last minute by the deeds of that stalwart of the world's highways – the cabbie!.Stand up and take a bow sir and/or madam!

No-one else in the world can so efficiently transport you to your place of abode, business or liaison quite like that trusted soul behind the taxi's wheel. And not only get you there but also enlighten you on the cure for all the world's ills, the state of the English cricket team and the way in which government, national health service and showbusiness should be run. And all this without prompting or even showing any interest in the subjects at all.

Ah – if only these good people would come out from behind their steering wheels and take over the leadership!.What a perfect world we would have then – heaven on earth!.Justice for all and the only worry – an eternally clicking meter!

I guess in our time we've all had a funny cab experience and I don't profess to have had funnier than you, but please pardon my listing a few that have happened to me and to others I know.

Let's take me - generally a car person A to B and little use for the cabbies' art. But just on occasion it makes an extremely pleasant change to sink into the back seat of a cab and leave it all to the expert.

So it was on a recent visit to my home town of Liverpool. Settled nicely in a hotel and car parked up for the weekend, I travelled to the Philharmonic Hall in the back of a black cab.

'How's it going, Tommy?' were the first words out of the driver's mouth. (Obviously he'd know where I was working and, checking the time, would know that's where I was headed.)

'Fine, mate,' I replied, 'Good to be back home, and see the town back on the up!'

'On the up? Liverpool? Nah!!.Not yet, Tommy,' he countered.

'Don't you think so?' I pressed, 'From what I've noticed lately the heads are getting high again and the laughter's getting louder!'

'No, Tommy, son. You're wrong there,' he persisted, 'This town is still on the floor!'

'Really?'

'Really!'

'In what way??'

'Well, Tommy, I'll tell you how bad Liverpool is – it's eight months since somebody's been sick in the back of this car!!'

Wow! Serious times, obviously, for my home town. Bad days still with us because, obviously, in the good old days he had to clean the back of the cab out every night!.Ah – the good times!.But such is the cabbies lot. Not all pleases him and not all can he put right. How infuriating. What a world.

Let me give you the instance of the Dublin taxi driver who picked me up at Jury's Hotel to take me to the airport.

'You know,' said he, as I had literally just entered the cab, 'You're not the first famous person I've ever carried!'

'I'm sure I'm not,' said I.

'Oh no!.I once took the legendary Dave Allen to the airport from this very hotel.'

'Nice man, Dave,' I mused.

'Not that nice,' insisted Padraig (for that was his name). 'In fact he was a little bit stroppy.'

'No ...' I smiled.

'Ah yes. Ah yes,' went on 'the man'.

'When he first got into the back, do you know what he said to me?'

'I can't begin to guess,' I smiled again.

'He said, 'Listen friend. Here's the deal. The journey is about twenty minutes and during it if you don't tell me any Irish jokes I won't tell you how to drive this car.' Now what do you think about that?' groaned Padraig.

'Maybe it was just a bad day,' I ventured. 'I'm sure he would have loved to hear you wit normally.'

'Maybe you're right,' said the man, 'Now you're the

kind of feller who could tell a good yarn. Do you know the one about Murphy ………….. ?'

'My God,' thought I, 'You've done it now. You've opened a vein. Dave Allen, sir, You've a lot to answer for!'

Of course, not all cab drivers are the same. A poorer world it would be if that were so. And it's certain that somewhere there exists the one driver who has no opinions, knows no jokes and wants no chatter whilst he works. Personally I've never met him but I've heard stories.

My pal, Wyn Calvin, comedian extraordinaire and the best panto dame in the business swears the following happened to him – and who am I to argue with a lady ,albeit baritone-voiced and hard as the Welsh mountains?

It was this way, or so Wyn would have it....   !.

The jolly Welshman was travelling from his Cardiff home to the railway station and the cabbie, well mannered and quiet of nature, was busy weaving his way through the early morning traffic – not in any particular hurry and enjoying the summer's day with driving window down and right elbow on the windowsill. Suddenly Wyn decided he might need reading matter on the train journey and tapped the driver on the shoulder to ask him to pull in at a newsagents. In the split second his fingers tapped the man's shoulder, he let out a piercing scream and, shoulders and arms flailing, lost control of the car shouting, 'Don't do that!!.Don't do that!'

'What?' shouted Wyn as the cab finally came to rest, lying almost sideways on across the road.

'Sorry, mate,' blustered the driver, 'But it's me first day driving a cab. For the last fifteen years I've been driving a hearse!'

Strange people you meet in Wales. But not just in Wales. We have them in Liverpool, too. Ask anyone – well, nearly anyone. Well, be sensible, why not go straight to the source. This I did and got two great stories. True or not – they should have been.

I tackled a Liverpool taxi driver and asked him to give me his best anecdotes and he came up with these beauties. A cab was called to Yates' Wine Lodge in Moorfields, Liverpool to 'pick up a fare who'll be waiting in the doorway!' When the cab arrived the driver spotted the potential customer swaying unsteadily in the evening air. Thoughts of the fare being sick and heralding the return of the good old days flashed through the cabbie's mind but he restricted himself to opening the back door and calling, 'Taxi?'

'Yeah,' mumbled the fare and, slumping into the seat and slamming the door, added, 'Yates' Wine Lodge, mate,' and promptly fell asleep, whereupon the quick thinking driver revved the engine, sat where he was for about three minutes, then released the handbrake, rolled five yards down the gentle slope and banged on his brakes.

''Ere y'are, pal,' he shouted.

'Wha?'

'We're here. Yates' Wine Lodge!'

'Humff,' came the voice from the rear, 'How much?'

'Call it three quid,' said the smiling cabbie.

'Here y'are – three quid,' mumbled the wino, 'And – next time, not so *****(blankety-blank) fast!!'

Ah – what a peril drunks can be, but the not-so-drunks and sobers can be a handful, too - especially the foreign ones. Eric Merriman's brother can vouch for that. Eric, a very fine writer of comedy scripts and songs gave me his brother's classic many years ago and, to date, it still holds its own as a top ten funny taxi tale.

Brother Jim was a black cab driver in Liverpool and his tale began when he returned from a fortnight's holiday to discover that his own cab was off the road with transmission problems.

'Take 65, Jim,' said the boss, 'Joe O'Leary's not in till Friday.'

So – off sped our hero to pick up his first fare – a Chinese seaman waiting at the gate of the Huskisson Dock on the Liverpool Dock Road. Pulling up alongside the sailor, Jim motioned to the rear door and said, 'Hop in pal,' whereupon the Chinaman disappeared into the back of the cab. Off set Jim, whistling his merry way along the cobbled road and waiting for instructions as to when to turn and where to go. Nothing – Zilch!.So rather tetchily he looked in the mirror to try to catch the seaman's eye – but alas and alack – no seaman!.The man had apparently vapourised. 'Maybe he fell out further back,' thought Jim. 'Nah!.I'd have heard the door slam.' But what other reason could there be? Thieves? Possible but improbable. Magic? The occult? A passing kidnapper? Only one way to start the search – stop the car and have a shufti.

This our hero began to do, opening the back door and being stopped dead in his tracks. Problem solved immediately – no abduction, just a patient smiling Chinese sitting on the floor of the taxi – but why?

Well apparently Joe O'Leary had complained about rattling and squeaking from the rear of the vehicle and the mechanics had removed the back seat to treat the problem and had simply forgotten to put it back. Our Asian friend, none the wiser, had entered the cab and assumed he had to sit on the bare floor, knowing nothing of the two flip-down seats that back on to the driver.

'Well,' smiled Jim,' He looked quite happy so I just

left him sitting there till we got to the destination.' Blimey. What a tale that Chinese would have to tell if he ever found out what really should be inside a British cab!.A funny tale of an unfortunate foreigner, but now a not-so-funny tale – well it wasn't when it happened to me.

Let's go back a few paragraphs to Jim Merriman looking in the mirror to catch the passenger's eye. Has that ever happened to you? It's certainly happened to me, with embarrassing results.

For my experience I have to call on that true bastion of all things British and humorous – the London cabbie. Here, in one person, is the personification of the world's only superhuman. A man of resounding intellect, staggering foresight, and unbounding energy. The complete expert on politics, sport (any one!), family affairs and economics. A man who, with one stroke, could alter the entire world for the better, but prefers to be seated in interminable traffic queues dispensing his superior knowledge out of the side of his mouth, over his shoulder to whoever may listen.

Ah yes – the man – the man of all men. Who knows what lies behind that knowing smile and carefree attitude? Who knows what ticks in that most agile of brains? Only the select few ever get to find out only once - and once only. It happened to me.

It was this way. My busy schedule (those were the days!) demanded that I work London's Grosvenor House Hotel one Monday evening and then fly to Edinburgh from Heathrow next morning. So, bouncing with health and 'full of the joys' I hopped into the back of a black cab whilst the hotel's concierge instructed the driver, 'Heathrow, mate.'

Off we sped and, for fear of awaking a sleeping giant, I chose to sit tight-lipped and enjoy the ride.

Soon, though, it became evident that my driver had developed a somewhat compelling curiosity. Each time we stopped at traffic lights or roundabouts I caught him staring at me in his rear view mirror. This went on, without a work spoken, for the whole of the journey. In the end it became quite embarrassing – so much so that I began to stare out of the window to escape his gaze. Finally the whole episode came to a head as we left the M4 motorway and dropped down to the traffic lights just outside the airport. Pulling up and staring straight at me in the mirror, the cabbie said, 'Go on then – give us a clue.'

'Oh,' I blushed, 'Tom O'Connor - Name that Tune, Crosswits … '

'No, no you prat" he snapped. 'Which terminal?'

Oh the shame!.Could anything be worse? You're darned right pal, and it happened to me. Honest!

Similar scenario to the last one – a taxi called to a hotel and the porter instructing the driver as to my destination, whilst I flopped back in my seat. Ah well – everything under control, no problems. Well – not until the cabbie glanced in his mirror and spotted me.

'Blimey, I didn't know it was you!' he smiled. 'Wait till I tell my mate John. He's your biggest fan, John is. Wait till I tell him!.Do you know why John thinks you're brilliant?! he asked.

'Can't guess! I muttered, knowing I was about to find out.

'John picked you up eleven years ago and you said you'd do your job for nothing because you loved it so much.'

'That still applies today,' I assured him.

'Cor – wait till John finds out you've been in my cab,' went on the driver.

''Ere,' he said, 'You wouldn't talk to him now would

you? Suddenly I had only two choices – Hobson's and none!

'All right,' I agreed and watched as John's mate dialed him up on his mobile.'John,' he almost shouted, 'You'll never guess who's in the back of my car,' - and with that he passed me the phone, saying, 'Don't tell John who you are. Let him guess.'

'Hello, John,' I said in my best Tom O'Connor voice, 'About eleven years ago you picked me up and I said I'd do my job for nothing because I loved it so much.'

'Naw,' said John, 'Haven't got you!'

'Tell him you've got the same first name as me,' prompted the cabbie.

'I've got the same first name as your pal,' I said.

'What – Terry?'Terry? Terry? Terry who???

Well, it took a while, quite a while actually to realize that these two lovely men thought I was Terry Griffiths, the snooker legend. And so, rather than break any hearts I played the game and talked snooker for twenty minutes – the longest cab trip I think I've ever been on. (Felt like a month!!)

Finally, journey's end arrived and, having bluffed my way through, I was at least heartened by the words, 'Thanks for being a great sport. Have this trip on me!'

Ah – the beauties of door to door travel. The unknown wonders that lie in store for the unsuspecting passenger. Ah the unpredictability of it all. Well, almost all. There are still, thank goodness, one or two cast iron certainties that pertain when dealing with the last of the gunfighters – Mr Cab Driver.

A long time ago I was given a poignant joke which still applies. It attempts to point out the difference between London and New York drivers.

In London you'd ask the taxi driver to help you put the pram in the boot of the vehicle. In New York you'd ask the cab driver to help you put the baby carriage in the trunk.

Actually it doesn't matter what you say as neither of them will help you anyway!!

The cabbie – the cabbie. Where would we be without the cabbie?

Don't answer that!.

Chapter 13

Fly me!

Isn't it funny that, as soon as you mention air travel everybody has a favourite story to tell - whether it happened to them personally or to a friend or, more obscurely, 'an acquaintance of a friend'?

Whatever the source, the tales of disaster, distress or even downright hysteria all have a similar ring. Lost luggage, late arrivals, engine trouble and so on.

These twentieth and twenty-first century plagues appear to have been sent to try us all. So it is difficult, when attempting to write a book on travel, to decide what to use, what to believe and, probably most importantly, what would make entertaining reading.

With this in mind I've spent more than enough time editing, re-editing and even totally re-writing this chapter in the hope that it comes out at least slightly different from others you've read. And, on the advice of a very well-read and talented man (my English teacher at St Mary's College, Crosby!) I've decided to 'start with a good 'un' just to get, and hopefully hold, your interest.

In my trade of jobbing comedian and all round jolly chap there are many who could in alcoholic-induced rantings claim to be 'the guvner'. None would be correct because the real 'guvner' would never, and need never, go in for crass self-promotion. The real 'top man' needs say nothing; his peers say it for him.

Ask any comic worth his salt who is 'the best in the business' and they will reply, 'Bob Monkhouse.' If that's good enough for everybody in the comedy business then a story from the master should be good enough for us as we trundle into our aeroplane chapter.

Bob has a pal called Nigel – Nigel Gaye, and Nigel is a devil for a bargain – cut price this, two for the price of one that, twenty per cent more for half the amount, etc – you know the kind of person – probably personally.

Well, the bold Nigel, on holiday in the US, found a cut-price flight from Seattle to Pennsylvania – basically a standby seat - for hardly anything. So, naturally, he booked one, irrespective of the fact that he had no reason to go to Pennsylvania – nor had he any desire to see any sights therein. Mr Gaye was driven only by the desire to 'save' money by travelling cheaply.

Pittance duly paid, our hero boarded the flight and was allocated Seat 1A. Hardly had he fastened his seat belt when the stewardess came to him and said, 'Apologies Mr Gaye, but another passenger who has paid full fare would like your seat because it's wide bodied. Is it possible you could move to 7B?'

'No problem,' smiled Nigel, 'No problem at all,' and he duly made his way back six rows. But the move was to have cataclysmic, though hysterical, results.

Right on the heels of the first stewardess came another, escorting two late 'runners' for the plane – two people who had paid full fare and so outranked our bargain-hunter.

The upshot of this was that Nigel was about to be asked to get off and wait for the next flight. However, the second lass didn't know that he had moved seats! So – she approached the man in 1A and said, 'Are you Gaye?'

'Yes,' he replied coyly.

'Then you'll have to get off!' she said. Nigel who couldn't let this go unchallenged shouted, 'I'm sorry, but you've got it wrong – I'm Gaye!'

'So am I,' came a voice from 9C. 'But they can't throw three of us off!!'

Ah – who would have thought in those very early days of flying that life would become so very complicated today. Men on the Moon, satellites in orbit, and chaos on earth. What went wrong? What happened to those lazy hazy days of air travel? How far do we have to go back to rediscover a time of sweetness and light and no problems? Was there ever such a period of aviation history?

Well, personally, I can go back to the 50s and, through a blur of fading memory and biased nostalgia, I recall my first experiences of travelling from Speke Airport Liverpool to Dublin in an Avro Anson plane – possibly a relic from World War Two – which was a wonder in its day but slightly less stable than a Jumbo jet.

It was sad that such a fine aircraft should have to bear the name of 'the milk plane' by Merseysiders. Apparently the legend was that the Dublin to Liverpool leg was used to transport crates of Irish milk across. In fact there were people, and some survive who swore that late at night they could hear the crates and bottles rattling as she flew overhead!

Wrongly nicknamed, the plane was still a fine sight to see and in fact be aboard. Perhaps the only blot on an otherwise awe-inspiring landscape was the weighing, not only of baggage but also passengers so, that the weight could be evenly distributed. This would totally irk my Dad who, at 20 stones, was always forced to sit on his own – generally opposite two ladies whose gross tonnage approximated his.

This apart, we all used to look forward to the flight. Despite the fact that turbulence was felt so much more in such an early machine it was nothing compared with the almost typhoon conditions that could be met when crossing on the ferry. Ah yes – those good old days of jam-free roads to the airport, no air traffic control problems, carrying your own luggage to the plane and overseeing its storage and retrieval. Gone they are, gone beyond recall, but the funny stories still live on – in memory and in round-the-fire (or TV) tales of yesteryear.

Let's stay in Liverpool for our next example. Thanks to their success in European football, Liverpool FC and, occasionally Everton FC, have spent many hours playing matches in foreign lands with mixed success. But remember that, easy as today's journeys are executed, there was a time when the organization was, to say the least, haphazard.

Take an early trip to Germany to play FC Cologne (the Everton fans used to say, 'You may have walked Hamburg but you'll never walk Cologne!') and a host of Liverpool FC fans descending upon Speke Airport.

No such thing then as automated ticketing and computerized baggage stowage. It was just a 'queue up and get on when and where you can' system – survival of the fittest or the largest; weight distribution a thing of distant memory. And so the lads, for they mostly were in those days, (few ladies would stand for the chaos) formed a three-deep crocodile which stretched from the plane's steps to the departure lounge. Each member of the never-ending file was regaled head to toe in red and white – hats, scarves, jerseys and favours with the still legal rattles. What a sight and what a source of humour.

Apparently in the midst of this shuffling throng, one red and white bedecked fan turned to another similarly garbed and asked, 'Are you going to the match?' What a way to get things off to a flying start, literally; but nothing, compared with what was in store at the other end.

Supposedly I'm led to believe, the arriving Scousers dutifully formed a queue at Passport Control and one more vociferous member of the chorus enquired of the German customs officer, 'Hey, pal – where's the nearest boozer?'

'You're looking at him,' came the reply. He'd been a prisoner of war in Manchester for four years!

True – or so they say. Well, no less true than the legendary tale of when, match won and Cologne pubs shut, bails paid and wounds tended, the Merseyside contingent returned to the airport in a vain effort to all be home first! Following basic instincts (and the bloke in front) about three hundred fans boarded a plane whose total capacity was about a hundred and twenty. Every seat was full. Some with two occupants! People were sitting cross-legged two abreast in the aisle, the loos contained upwards of half a dozen each. No way to run a railway or an airline! And this fact was swiftly made known by the pilot.

'Come on boys. There are too many of you – it's not safe. We're too heavy to take off – we literally can't do anything till some of you get off.'

'What'd he say?' asked a bloke near the back and far from a speaker.

'Plane's not safe!' shouted one who could hear.

'Not safe!' mumbled around two hundred voices. 'Not safe!' came the cry from each throat as everybody literally got up, got off the plane, and got on the one behind!

I'm assured it happened at least once. It may have happened any number of times, maybe not. But for sure something delayed the boys' return by at least six hours.

'Terrible fog, love,' some explained to their long-suffering wives and partners.

'Helping Interpol with an international manhunt,' others tried. Whatever, it would be a long time before peace was restored to Merseyside homes and the suffering of 'the silent treatment' would cease.

But at least when our rambling boys returned they were still in possession of all their belongings – if not their faculties.

Sad is the traveller (yeah, verily sad) who ends a journey with less than he started. Remember the old saying about Concorde and its speed of sound speed – 'Breakfast in London, lunch in New York, luggage in Hong Kong?'

Funny, yes, but did it ever happen to you? It did? Not that hysterical is it? It happened to me, in a smallish way, when I decided to fly from Glasgow to Inverness on the 'highlands and islands' plane. Having finished a Sunday show early and returning to my pantomime in Inverness I checked in my suitbag at Glasgow Airport and boarded the eight-seater plane.

Immediately after take-off the cabin steward, I swear wearing an overcoat and gloves! – came to me and said, 'The pilot wants to see you immediately.'My God,' I thought, 'He's had a heart attack and knows I used to fly!' I did, but not for very long – no Biggles me!

On reaching the cockpit the Skipper motioned me to

sit beside him and asked,

'Did you check in a bag at Glasgow?'

'Ye-e-es,' I replied with, I'm sure, the most quizzical look on my face.

'I thought it was you, because the other passengers are regulars and wouldn't do that!' he said.

'So, what are you saying then?' I pressed.

'Well, in a word,' he grinned, 'Your bag is on a shuttle going to Heathrow.'

'But,' I spluttered, 'Never mind the inconvenience, what about the security aspect?'

'Listen, mate,' said the Skipper, 'You think that's bad. We had a bloke coming up to Perth and his luggage went to Australia!!'

And do you know, I was not surprised because I'd heard a similar story that happened in Ireland when the initialled luggage tags were first introduced.

You know LHR – London Heathrow, etc. It's said that bags travelling from Cork to Dublin (Dub) were carefully dispatched to Dubai.

Ah – the miseries, the unknown quantities, the laughter and the tears – but it's all part of the grand design which we call 'getting from here to there'.

Let me treat myself to a chapter of my own....

Chapter 14

You couldn't make it up!

Remember those classic TV shows 'Candid Camera', 'Beadles About', and the like? Did you ever wonder what went through the minds of the poor souls who were tricked and laid bare to public ridicule?

Did you ever begin to suspect that you were being set up – did paranoia set in? It did with me on more than one occasion, the latest being one of the most bizarre.

I was flying to Barbados, accompanied by my wife and my witness, and two hours into the journey the cabin crew were taking orders for the evening meal. In the row in front of us were two charming ladies with North American accents, probably American but possibly Canadian.

As the American Airlines' stewardess hove into view the lady on the right enquired, 'There's a choice of lamb or fish cakes?'

'Yes, madam,' came the reply.

'Could you tell me if there's any seafood in the fish cakes?' As I sat stunned and looking for video cameras, the conversation went on.

'I'm not sure madam, I'll go and find out.'

I looked around and realized that the only people reacting to the exchange were Pat and me. Maybe the rest of the passengers had witnessed similar exchanges before, but nevertheless it's a little disconcerting even though I'd had one almost as comical on a flight to Nairobi. We joined a Kenya Airways plane at Heathrow. First class tickets had been provided and we made our way forward to find only one other passenger in our cabin – a very nice Egyptian gentleman.

After the formalities of safety drill, take off, and climb to cruising height we were greeted by our cabin stewardess who was taking orders for lunch. She went to our Egyptian friend first – and then to me.

'Choose one of these,' she half-ordered and shoved the menu at me. It had been handwritten, probably by herself, and offered two choices – Beef or Ostrich steak.

Ever the gambler I asked for the ostrich. 'We've got none left,' came the curt reply. So I was left to work out for myself that there had been one portion and the Egyptian had ordered it. Nonetheless, I was happy just to be in first class and whilst awaiting the beef I decided to recline my seat and have a nap. While the seat was in the half way back position and still moving, the arm fell off!

What to do? What to do indeed! Being British I had no choice but to hastily clip it back on and hold it in place – wouldn't you? Because we'd rather die than make a fool of ourselves!

Something happened to my pal, Paul! Paul – Cockney and 'praaad' of it, perpetual motion on legs, sell anything to anyone, fix stuff that isn't 'broke' – and a good mate, was travelling to Cyprus with his good lady Audrey.

On boarding the plane, and not being enamoured

with flying, he was ushered to an aisle seat – handy for an emergency – where he 'belted up' and tried to settle himself in the best way possible considering the lack of leg room. During his writhings, Paul sensed that all was not well with his seat – it seemed to rattle about at every movement of his body. In fact, the whole thing appeared to be unstable.

''Scuse me love,' he called to a passing stewardess, 'This seat ... er,' but she was gone!

'Here, mate,' he tried on an obviously uninterested steward, 'I think I might have ... ' gone again'

'Can someone 'elp me 'ere?' came the cockney bellow from an irate Paul, 'I fink I'm in trouble with this bleeding seat.'

'What is matter?' queried the cabin purser, a lass of East European origin.

'This chair, love - it aint right.'

'Well, wait until we are in air and I will find you another seat,' she assured him. 'Now sit still and wait for take-off.'

Having been duly admonished Paul and Audrey sat back as best they could and listened attentively to the safety drill – making double certain where the emergency exits were – just in case.

In no time at all, the plane was racing along the runway and beginning its jet-powered climb skywards. All was well, or appeared to be, at least until the plane reached an angle of about 30 degrees to the horizontal, whereupon, whatever was holding Paul's seat to the fuselage gave way and he, still belted tightly, and the whole seat, came adrift and rolled down the plane like a bowling ball, clattering passengers and fittings alike in its mad dash towards the rear.

'Sorry mate! Oops – sorry love.! 'Can't 'elp it dear.'

These were some of the more printable phrases

which came from my mate's lips. In fact, in his rearward careerings and concern for others he'd almost completely forgotten the pain and injuries he himself was suffering.

On levelling out of course all hands rushed to help the human cannonball – tea and alcoholic beverages were proffered but Paul was more interested in compensation!

'Ruined our holiday you have,' he remarked as panic left him and aitches returned to his vocabulary.

'You should pay for this, you know!' And they did - hospitalisation, traction and all.

Still, it was amusing, and still is when recalled, to see my friends return from a fortnight in the sun – Audrey as brown as a berry all over, and Paul with sunburned fingertips – the only part of him that had not been swathed in bandages.

Now from one 'casualty' aboard a plane to another - although the circumstances were slightly different. Well, for a start, Paul is mid-forties, the other 'injured' party was at least mid-eighties. A charming lass who'd travelled aboard P&O's Oriana for the duration of one leg of a world cruise. About two weeks out at sea there was sun, fun and loads to nibble at – not to mention the booze! Not to mention? I'm sorry but I have to; it's the crux of the story and I was there to see it!

Elsie, for it was she, was on the same flight as I was from Panama City to good old Blighty. She'd bought her quota, and a little more, of alcohol and tobacco whilst still at sea and they were safely stowed in her suitcases in the hold of the Jumbo. But – on settling into her seat and having enjoyed a super meal and a few, sorry several, jars she enquired about duty-free sales. These arrived and were safely placed in the overhead compartment.

Loose-lipped, this Lancashire lady began to open up about all the other 'bits and pieces' she'd accrued on her 'voyage of a lifetime' – leaving us all wondering what might happen if the customs and excise fronted her up and searched her bags.

'Poor soul would have a heart attack,' I thought. But I was wrong – well, at least about the timing.

You see, Elsie had the heart attack before she went through customs. In fact she flaked out literally as the plane landed. The timing was split-second. Grabbing her chest and foaming at the mouth she slumped in her seat, just as the door opened.

'Quick, notify a doctor – wheelchair immediately. Stretcher would be better!' was the buzz as we all looked on half sad, half bewildered.

Gently and efficiently the paramedics stretchered her off, placing her duty-free on her chest, whilst provisions were being made to transfer her cases direct to her home.

'Funny,' said a man two rows behind me. 'It's like she knew exactly what she was doing.'

'Not half,' chirped the lady who'd boarded with her. 'She does it every time!'

Who'd have thought? Who'd have believed? We all should have. Brothers and sisters, we should never stop believing because the more we see and hear, the more we realize how strange is life - and how much stranger are people.

Haven't we all had a moment in our lives when the world and its wonders take over events and the whole shebang seems to carry on without our help, or even our 'by your leave'? Like it or not we are dragged along in a merry free wheel that always ends in a surprise twist that could never be predicted. It's probably happened many times to all of us, but it still comes as a complete shaker when it does.

I suppose it's difficult to pick one particular moment to stand out from the rest but I like to think I've managed it. The setting being Ireland, at least you are half prepared for what is to come. When it involves air travel it whittles it down even more.

It was 1991 and I was due to appear in pantomime at the Opera House, Belfast. A fine script an excellent cast and costumes aplenty! All, it seems, we were short of was some good publicity. No bother. The local press, radio and TV were only too willing to oblige and assist – an entertainer's dream!

One of the company, playing the fairy godmother and playing it well, was lovely Candy Devine a talented actress, vocalist and DJ. Candy had her own show on Downtown Radio and suggested that we appear together to chat about old times and plug the panto – great idea!

Duly ensconced in the studio, we were to follow the eleven o'clock news bulletin. We did but not quite in a fit state. The main item of news was that a scheduled flight from England was coming in to land at Belfast City airport and was being talked in by Ground Control. Suddenly the plane disappeared from the radar screens and mild panic set in.

'Hotel Whiskey, where are you?' cried the radar operator.

'I'm down,' said the pilot.

'No, you're not.'

'Look, pal. I'm in the thing. I know where I am. I'm on the ground.'

'We can't see you,' said Ground Control.

'Trust me. I'm here,' stressed the pilot. Suddenly a brainwave!!

'Hotel Whiskey, what can you see?'

'Horses and cows,' came the reply.

What neither had realised was that the pilot had missed the airport altogether and had landed at a disused RAF base some miles away. But now came the problem.

Because the runway was too short to take off again the plane was stranded. So, how to get the passengers off?

'Easy,' thought the pilot, and fired the escape chutes. Now he had the passengers on the ground minus their luggage!

When this knowledge set in the Captain was last seen being chased across the tarmac by a hundred and odd passengers waving umbrellas and handbags and threatening to 'break his head'.

As this scene sank in back at the studio my mind began to race.

'If the plane can't take off again,' I thought out loud, 'How will they get it back to the main airport?'

'Easy,' replied Candy,' They'll take the wings off and tow it back by road.'

'How do you know that?' I asked in amazement.

Candy smiled and said, 'Because that's what they did last time!'

… For me an unforgettable moment – and I'm delighted to say that in my life I've had quite a few of those.

Chapter 15

It's a funny world

There's an old adage, 'Cometh the hour, cometh the man'. It's been used about historical legends from David and Goliath to Frances Drake, to Winston Churchill. You won't find any particular hero in any history book or chronicle but he in his town was as important to me as any of the others. Major Peter Ball, I salute you, sir. You led this weary traveller and his spouse out of the jaws of uncertainly into the light and beyond.

It was the early nineties and cruising holidays were becoming the rage – as indeed they are to this day. Leading the charge towards excellent value and fine seamanship was my all time favourite liner – Canberra. Ah – where is she now? What would we pay for just one more voyage?

Being a regular entertainer aboard it became a minor perk as to which trips I should take and where and when I should get on and off. Having seen most of the world it came down to – where next? Well, what about Panama City? I'd been through the canal – a stunning experience – but never stayed in the city itself. Here was my chance. So Pat and I duly disembarked at the port town of Crystobal and headed for our hotel.

We had all that day and overnight to spend sampling the delights of South American hospitality. Fed and watered finely in the hotel restaurant, we were browsing around the lobby shop when a gentleman approached.

'I think you're famous or something, aren't you?' he asked. Great question.

'Sort of,' I replied with a smile.

'My daughter would know. She watches TV,' I was assured.

'I do do a little of that,' I said modestly.

'Well, good luck to you, lad; more power as they say.'

And off he went. Nice man, well dressed to the point of elegance – obviously ex-military with his bearing. What was he now? Diplomat? Businessman? Spy? What?

'I'd love to see his passport details,' I thought and smiled at the old gag about the royal retainer holidaying in Australia. At immigration the customs official read the passport and, pausing where it said, 'occupation – courtier,' looked up and said, 'There's no 't' in courier mate!'

But, back to the plot. We spent our evening enjoying a meal of fish fare and thorougly enjoyed the humid conditions which prevail in those exotic South American lands. We also more than enjoyed meeting a middle-aged lady from Blackpool.

It was no accident that our paths crossed, just clever deduction by Pat. The lady in question sat all alone in the warm tropical night with only a glass of lager as companion. But it was her dress that gave away her British roots; thick tweed suit, thick grey tights and brogue shoes – and a huge necklace of huge beads that seemed to be there solely to catch the beads of sweat which pumped from her brow.

'God knows the state of her armpits,' I thought, but .... 'Good evening – you're British aren't you?' was what I actually said.

'Yes, Blackpool and fed up.'

'What's the problem?' I asked as if I couldn't guess.

'Him,' she said, 'Him.'

'He' apparently was the husband, in disgrace and banished to the bedroom.

'I married a clown,' she went on, 'And I've only just realized it.'

'Can't be too bad,' I assured her.

'Too bad!' Too bad!' She almost screamed, attracting the attention of more than half the residents. 'I'll tell you how bad if you like! You see, we're market traders and we deal in everything. You name it we sell it. Everything at bargain price – that's his way of thinking – even this holiday.'

'Well .... ' I ventured.

'Hang on,' she said, 'Hang on!' Wait'll you hear this. He packed for the ten day stay here in Panama and when we got to our hotel room and opened up the three cases, they were all full of yellow dusters! That's why I'm still dressed like I was when we left Manchester Airport!'

Apparently their house is an Aladdin's Cave of stock for the market stall – including dozens of suitcases each full of different commodities. Poor disgraced hubby had picked up the wrong three!!

We spent the late evening chuckling at their distress and wondering when, if ever, they eventually made it up. But such things are what world travel is made up of; human disasters which spring from nowhere, as we were to learn to our own cost the following morning!

Isn't there always something odd that gives away the confusion at airports? Something not quite right – do you know what I mean? Something that could easily go unnoticed were it not for the fact that you're an experienced traveller?

At Panama City airport it was the fact that people were checking in, discharging their luggage and receiving boarding passes with no seat numbers on. I'd seen this once before in Italy and then it was because the flight was overbooked. This time it turned out the problem was even worse; not that we noticed. That was left to the man of the moment – looming like John Wayne out of the mist.

'Whatever you do, don't check in your bags,' boomed the Stentorian voice,

'Something isn't right here,'

It was Peter Ball, world traveller and possible spy, who arrived just in time to lighten our burden.

'You,' he said loudly in the general direction of the two hapless souls behind the first class booking desk, 'Bring me the manager immediately.'

And in a flurry of sweat and feathers a gentleman duly arrived.

'Speak English?' enquired the Major.

'Que,' replied the gentleman.

'No good, no good,' said Peter. 'He can't be the manager if he can't speak English!' (What a wonderfully British line!) 'Bring me someone who can, and give me a copy of the A to Z of flying – there, that one on the shelf.'

Whilst an English speaking 'manager' was being sought, our saviour had discovered that the scheduled flight to London was suffering engine trouble and could be laid up for days – even a week – not funny. So on the appearance of an airline agent of far-Eastern origin with fluent English, the order was given in the way that only a British major could.

'I want three first class seats on the next plane going East. I think you'll find it's an Iberian flight at 10.05 am tomorrow. I also want a note from you saying your airline will cover our hotel bills for this evening. Please book two hotel rooms and order us a cab if you will.'

And do you know what? The man did! Before the other 300 would-be passengers even discovered the state of the plane we were ensconced in five-star luxury and begging Peter Ball to let us treat him to a meal.

'No, no. Busy day tomorrow. Two Mogadon and an early night for me. See you tomorrow,' he smiled and disappeared.

Wow – what a man. Car in the morning to the airport – first class travel to Madrid. He'd even arranged our onward tickets to Heathrow and a porter to transport the luggage from one terminal at Madrid to the other.

'Don't tip him – I've done it!' were the last words we heard him say before he was swallowed up by the throng.

Wherever you are today, my dear major, good luck and good health, and whichever roads you take, may one of them lead you back to me so I may thank in deed as I have many times in prayer.

Yes, indeed. Even in today's computerized world where all is automation and plastics, it is still possible to find characters, although some may have been better undiscovered. I'm sure, dear reader, you've met the type – pessimists, rainers on parades, stick in the muds and - Lord preserve us - practical jokers, who are surely the worst of all!

All right. We've all done it in our time. A silly jape, a

funny wheeze – an apple pie bed (you know, where the sheets are half-folded in the middle and a tired soul can't understand why he/she can't stretch out!). Knocking on front doors and running away (not recommended over the age of ten) disruptive e-mails – Mister Angry phone messages. Yes, we've done 'em but not so's they would cause real distress. Just for a laugh.

Like me in New York for the first time. Up for any sort of jape I purchased a tee-shirt which bore the logo, 'Don't tell me what kind of day to have!' This guaranteed to nonplus any barman, sales agent or waitress who churried out the usual, 'Have a nice day' line – delivered by rote like times tables.

It worked but didn't feel right – so I abandoned it. Basically no harm done but what about 'japes' that really can upset a person.

Take the pilot of the Canadian airliner (well on its way and at cruising altitude) who came on the microphone to say, 'Very shortly I shall be coming amongst you for a chat and to answer any questions you may have. Meantime my friend Harry will take over the controls,' and clicked off.

There was a five-second pause before the mike clicked on again and he added, 'Does anyone else have an invisible friend called Harry?'

Quiet panic and heavy whispering followed. The joke was neither seen, nor appreciated. A good dressing-down and threats of the sack, and worse, were to follow.

The pilot had an imaginary friend called Harry. I have a real flesh and bones friend called Eric. Eric is an amazing man, one of the most intelligent people I've ever met. Good golfer – great company – fine talker, but boy, what a prankster.

Never quite reaching the annoying stage, a lot of his

antics are, in themselves, totally harmless providing the people suffering have a reasonable sense of humour. But, there again, there are certain things that even a sense of humour can't forgive and I honestly didn't know that Eric was capable of such behaviour. Not, that is, until I met a pal of his who'd flown on many a mission with him in the 'good old days'.

Apparently the two had been pilots in the days of propeller-driven craft which were noisier, less comfortable and generally less reliable than today's graceful 'birds.' I rarely flew in those days and so never noticed whether the pilots wore uniforms or not. It seems that there was a certain relaxed attitude towards dress, providing a smart jacket and tie were worn.

Of course, in the smaller, possibly eight or ten seater planes the Captain would sit in almost full view of the passengers and here's where Eric took advantage.

When there was not a full compliment Eric would board, as if a smartly attired Passenger, and take a seat amongst the others. As time went by with no sign of anyone taking the controls, Eric would start the 'revolution'!

'I can't believe we're being kept waiting,' he'd mutter.

'Yes indeed,' someone would say.

'It's not right keeping first class passengers waiting this long, is it?' he'd ask.

'No, it certainly isn't,' more than one would reply.

'I'm sick to death of this lack of consideration.'

'Hear, hear,' would come the chorus.

'I'll tell you what,' Eric would say to a now totally rapt audience, 'If the pilot isn't here in two minutes I've a good mind to fly the thing myself.'

Smiles and knowing glances would be exchanged between the listeners. What a funny idea. Yes, very droll. Very droll indeed.

'Droll?' well yes. At least up to the point when Eric would rise from his seat, mutter something like, 'That does it. That does it,' and head for the controls, sit down and begin to fire the engines. Amazingly, so I'm told there would never be one voice raised in objection. Rather like the British that we are, the good folk at Eric's rear would sit, totally stunned (gob-smacked, banjaxed, or call it what you may) totally unable to produce a word of protest.

Large gins and tonics generally soothed the nerves after the joke was revealed. When enough had been quaffed there would be conversations like,

'I spotted it in the early stages you know, but I just wanted to go along with it.'

'So did I – but a good gag nonetheless.'

'Same with me,' – etcetera, etcetera.

Such banter, combined with the gin, usually saved Eric from reprimand, or at the worst, redundancy. Some joker, eh?

But, on reflection Eric was only a beginner in the trickster business – merely a babe in arms compared with others.

Let me round off this chapter with a classic story told to me by a British Airways purser whom I met whilst flying up to Glasgow. She was off-duty and going home for a day and, fortunately, was in a chatty mood.

'I'm writing a book on travel and its funny side. Any chance of a story from the other side to go with the numerous passenger tales I'm including?' I asked more in hope than in expectation.

'Well – there is one … ' she began, and then unloaded a most amazing anecdote on me.

It seems that there was a flight (airline unknown) travelling out of London to Miami. Take off and climbing to cruise height went like clockwork and an hour and a half out all was terribly well. Then, not unusually, a passenger in business class pressed the call button to attract a stewardess.

'Yes, sir?' she enquired.

'Look, miss,' said the middle-aged businessman, 'I don't want to cause a panic or anything, but I think the man next to me has just died. I've been around a lot of dead bodies and I'm pretty sure he's gone.'

Quickly informing the Captain of the conversation, the stewardess scanned the manifest for the presence of a doctor aboard. Sure enough there was one - a charming Indian gentleman who confirmed that he was indeed a doctor of medicine.

Duly he examined the passenger in question and confirmed that the man was deceased.

'Look,' said the businessman who had reported the incident, 'You can leave him there as far as I'm concerned. I know he's dead, I've had a sleeping pill and it doesn't worry me.'

The pilot, though, had different ideas. 'If we leave the man in his seat and rigor mortis sets in we may never get him out.'

So it was decided to remove the body to the coolest part of the plane, the rear galley. And so we have the classic case of two gay cabin stewards manfully trying to drag a corpse through business class - and then economy - being watched by dozens of pairs of eyes and open mouths.

The suspense was, too much for one of the stewards who, for devilment only, delivered the gold-medal line, 'Did anyone else have the fish?'

Let's draw a veil on the inquest into that story.

Chapter 16

Motor mania

No matter how you try – and I've tried hard – when writing about travel eventually, like it or no, the subject has to come around to motor cars, automobiles, coupes, hard tops, soft tops – man's (and woman's) best and worst friends.

Ah – the car, the car, given to us by the devil for all the best heavenly reasons. Comfort, ease of passage, speed, convenience, luxury – all are to behold when studying the publicity blurb or manufacturers' manual or TV ads.

The garden of Eden revisited, Shangri-la, the end of the rainbow – all are there under the roof, bonnet and boot (or hood and trunk for the Americans);a feast of fine living and easy driving for all – providing we can supply the original spark – money, lucre, greenbacks, folding stuff. No problem. Well, almost no problem. You see, in the auto-market all money, large or small amounts, is welcome.

The larger the amount the more luxurious the purchase, or vice versa. When listening to the rich man trilling the virtues of his latest limousine –'Overhead cam, BSS, ARS, ARP, ABC, XYZ' and so on and so on ... zzz!! It can possibly give a wrong impression. So too, of course, can listening to the under-spender.

'An old car – so old the log book's in Latin! One previous owner – Ben Hur; two-tone – dirt and rust.'

Ah the car, the car. What twists and turns it can lead us through and yet what a range of services it can provide – at least on paper. Multipurpose for family transport, two-seater for the poseur and Mr Smooth, Stretch limo for the already comfortable, a roof and some doors for those who don't care, a chariot to take us from A to B or even further.

The design, cost and upkeep of such a chariot depends literally on how we want to get there and at what speed and in what comfort and, most importantly of all, in what degree of safety. All this and heaven too – our own particular heaven, our own particular relief from the stresses and strains of life.

Well, that's the hard sell over with. Now let's get down to some hard facts!!

Apparently it really is a fact that traffic in London is now travelling at a much slower average speed than it did in the times of Queen Victoria and the horse-drawn carriages of her reign and before. Why should this be? Well, pick any answer from a hundred. Traffic lights? Narrow streets? Too many cars? – or the number one hate of any motorist – road works?

The man who invented the cone was probably knighted. If there was any justice in Britain he should have been crowned, preferably by a very strong man wielding a cone!

Ah yes – retribution indeed, but not an answer to the mighty travel problems that a driver meets every day.

I can recall appearing on a Royal Variety Show in

1977 to commemorate the Queen's 25th Anniversary. Roger de Courcey the ventriloquist asked Nookie his bear buddy, 'Are you having a street party to honour the Queen?'

'Yes, sir,' replied the furry one, 'We're having a party six and a half miles long.'

'Six and a half miles?' gasped Roger.

'Yes, sir,' said the bear, 'You know that lane of the M1 that's always closed? We're having it there!'

Blow me. Funny, yes – but still true today!

So why do we do it? Why do we scrimp and save to buy a car, spend hours cleaning it, spend even more hours trying to get it to a destination whilst still in charge of our senses and then spend even longer sometimes trying to park the thing? Because it's fun! Didn't anyone tell you that? Fun! Fun! Fun! Macabre maybe – but fun just the same.

Without the automobile we wouldn't have stories like the traffic warden who died and, as they were lowering his coffin into the grave, the mourners could hear him banging on the lid and shouting, 'Don't bury me – I'm not dead!'

'It's too late, mate,' said the vicar solemnly, 'We've already done the paperwork!'

Yes! Yes! One for the good guys. That's the reason we like the world of 'horseless carriages' – it's because of the funny stories we can relate.

To the lad or lass behind the wheel it seems that the world is totally and perpetually against them. No parking signs, no entry signs, no right turns, no left turns, one way systems, traffic light boxes, speed restrictions, breathalysers, speed cameras – why it just seems that Satan in all his glory has been left in charge of oppressing the poor oiks who pay inflated road taxes, huge insurance premiums and massive purchase tax and VAT on cars.So surely, it is only natural for the oppressed to retaliate in kind, and glory in the winning of even one small victory.

Take the classic tale of the late night traveller proceeding along the deserted M3 motorway at 105 mph in the early hours of Sunday morning, when he was overtaken and pulled over by a police car.

'Evening, sir,' said the bobby hitching up his trousers, (a sure sign of trouble on the way!) 'Burning quite a bit of rubber, weren't we?' (The royal 'we' confirms that trouble is certainly due.) 'Any reason why we'd be going so fast?'

'Well, officer,' came the reply, 'I was simply trying to keep up with the flow of traffic.'

'But there's nothing else on the road,' exclaimed Mr Plod.

'See,' smiled the motorist, 'I've lost them already!'

Cue either a smile and a caution or the wrath of hell – depending on the state of the liver of the law.

Who'd have imagined stories like these or, better still, the body in the boot saga (you must remind me to tell you that one later in the chapter) when we first ventured out on our first self-propelled trip in a car? When we look back to our driving roots and remember those stumbling early days of lessons and endless advice, cajoling from frustrated instructors or, worse still, relatives;the days when it all seemed totally beyond us; the feeling of envy that people who were obviously our intellectual juniors could drive and we couldn't. Or to paraphrase it, 'If that twit can do it, why can't I?'

You see, I was lucky. My instructor was a fine gentleman and excellent driver called Jimmy McCoy. Jimmy lived next door and worked for an undertaker (yes, I know you think there's a gag coming but no!). He started me off in quite a novel way, making me buy a car first and then challenging me to learn to manipulate the thing. All right, he was a little more heroic than that. I was in a musical duo and Jimmy was our road manager, running us from club to club and receiving a third of our wages as his fee and petrol outlay.

'You could save an awful lot,' he said one day, 'If you could drive yourself and cut me out.' Was there ever such selfless thinking? And so it was that, armed with the princely sum of £200 I bought my first motorized steed from an acquaintance of the McCoys, a missionary priest who'd had the car from new, two years old and in perfect nick – a more honest car dealer surely there has never been! And young O'Connor slid in behind the wheel of RDJ 705 – a bright yellow, sit up and beg Ford Popular car, 1962 vintage, eight thousand miles on the clock, three gears, top speed about 65 mph, wind-assisted, and the pride of Hornby Road, Bootle – the place where Pat and I set up home.

In 1964 it was a great place to be and a great era to be in; Mersey beat, mini skirts, mini cars, everything swinging and no worries; even a flippant outlook to cars and driving.

Who remembers being able to buy back-window stickers that looked like bullet holes? Who recalls getting a dent or bend in the body work and writing 'ouch' beside it in indelible ink? You do? So do I! We're old but gold, you and I, and we've been there and back.

But let me also admit the younger reader to the enclave and compare notes on things that happened to us all in our early motoring years - the first lesson; that moment when it became clear as crystal that you would never (in a year of Sundays, never mind a month) be able to control two hands, one wheel, two feet and three pedals at the same time – not forgetting indicators and

windscreen wipers – and the odd blast on the horn. Ah
– the horn!

How many times did other road users honk it madly
in your direction? Didn't you just hate that? Wouldn't
you just have loved to .... ah well, never mind. Back
to the script.

Back to the first time we released the clutch and
began our first solo trip – for surely every trip is solo.
Even with an accompanying instructor we're still in
sole charge of proceedings. It's entirely up to us
whether we proceed as our minds and limbs dictate or
whether we heed cries of anguish such as, 'Dip the
clutch now,' – 'Left hand down' – 'Brake ... Brake!!!'

The fact that we're still here proves we obeyed the
right instructions or were dead lucky. Either way it soon
became an exciting prospect to rise each day and
literally travel anywhere we liked. The freedom of the
open road lay before us and the world (well, at least the
A-road section!) was our oyster.

Too soon we became the person we are today –
totally forgetful of the days gone by – the driving test
we passed first time – or in my case, second time.

Due to an early timing chain fault in RDJ 705 I
performed an emergency stop and then couldn't start
again, the examiner refusing to give me a push start
even downhill and with the help of a passing milkman.

But those days are gone now, to be replaced by a life
of more mundane things such as power-steering,
advanced braking systems and air conditioning.
Quadraphonic sound, built-in telephones, satellite
navigation and turbo chargers have replaced the simple
pleasures of in-car fun. I can remember when 'deluxe'
after the name (Ford Prefect Deluxe) merely meant the
vehicle had a heater! (And not a very powerful one at
that.)

But it's different now. Now we're almost on automatic pilot when we go out. We have no in-car worries – now all our cares are outside the vehicle. More of that in the next chapter, but to close this one here's the 'body in the boot' tale for what it's worth.

A car travelling exceedingly quickly on the motorway was pulled over by a police patrolman.

'Do you realize you were exceeding 120 mph sir?'

'No, officer. I'm terribly sorry but I was in a hurry.'

'Really,' said the policeman with raised eyebrows, 'Why, sir, may I ask?'

'I was trying to escape.'

'Escape?'

'Yes, from the scene of the crime.'

'Crime?'

'Yes, where I stole this car.'

'Stole the car?'

'Yes. I'm heading for the river.'

'River?'

'To get rid of the gun.'

'Gun?'

'The gun in the glove compartment. I used it to shoot the bloke.'

'Shoot the bloke?'

'The owner of the car.'

'Owner?'

'Yes. I've got his body in the boot.'

'Wait … a minute,' gasped the lawman.

'Stolen car? Gun in the glove box? Body in the boot? Stay there while I call in some back-up.'

Duly called, and duly arrived, the back-up of armed officers was headed by a rather snappy inspector.

'Now, sir. You stole this car?'

'Not me,' said the driver, 'This is my car. Here's my documents. Here's my receipt of purchase. Here's a picture of me and the wife standing beside it.'

'But the officer said you'd stolen the car. OK – so what about the gun?' he went on.

'Gun?'

'In the glove compartment.'

'Sorry, Inspector, there's no gun in there. The glove box is empty. Have a look for yourself.'

And so it proved.

'The officer said you had a gun in there,' muttered the top cop glaring in the direction of PC1.

'OK,' he persisted, 'Let's see the body.'

'Body?'

'The one in the boot.'

'There's nothing in there except a spare wheel. Have a look for yourself.'

And that's all that was found – a spare wheel and wheel brace.

'I can't believe this,' shouted an almost apoplectic inspector. 'The officer said you stole the car, shot a man, put the gun in the glove box and put the body in the boot.'

'Go on,' smiled Mr Motorist,' I bet he told you I was speeding as well!'

Wow! What a story. Even if it's not all true. What another apocryphal tale for the good guys!

Chapter 17

It's better by car!

I suppose it's easy for us now to forget the days of insecurity behind the wheel when every move we made seemed to be wrong. When every suggestion made to us felt like a knife in the ribs.

I remember giving Pat her first (and in my case only) lesson, when she failed to depress the clutch to engage second, and we were hopping kangaroo-like down a quiet Yorkshire street. I called out in anguish, 'Dip the clutch, why don't you? Dip the clutch for God's sake!'

She replied equally loudly, 'Shut up. What do you know?' That did it. Lesson over. Professional instructor engaged. Funny, though, in retrospect.

But all that is now behind us and we've time to reflect, or even gloat on the distance we have travelled, literally and mentally in the time since. Time to sit back and regale others with our deeds, and misdeeds, behind the wheel. The speeds we've achieved, the scrapes we've survived, the good, the bad and the ugly motorists we've been behind or overtaken or just plain avoided.

I like the story of the little girl who said, 'Daddy, I went for a drive with mummy this morning and we never saw one stupid, nebulous prat all day!'

Yes, we've time to remember with fondness our time at the controls – the adventures that only motorized transport can lead a person to; the fun that even getting lost can bring.

Haven't we all got a 'losing the way' story to tell? Haven't we ourselves or a close friend or relative experienced the 'asking the way' saga?

'Looking for St Martin's church, mate.'

'You're not far. Go up this road and turn left where the dry cleaner's used to be!'

That's a cracker – or – 'Excuse me, love, do you know the Watford turn-off?'

'Yes – I married him!'

Two that happened to me have found their way into my act.

One cold Winter's evening I proceeded to Rochdale, Lancashire to perform at the Gracie Fields Theatre. (Beautiful theatre, beautiful lady.) It being an awkward place to find I enquired of a local in the main street, 'Where's the Gracie Fields theatre?'

'I'm not sure,' he replied, 'But go down to the cemetery and ask someone there!'

Little did I know that the cemetery was a pub situated in, of all places, Bury Road. Funny, but not my all-time best.

That would have to belong to a town not a million miles from Rochdale – a town in Greater Manchester called Higher Blackley.

There it was, on an equally dismal Winter's night, that I had been engaged to perform at the British Legion Club. Sadly nobody could tell me exactly where the venue was.

'It's near Manchester,' was the best guess. Oh no, it isn't! Not by a mile or three! But, of course, I didn't know that then.

So – accompanied by my pal, Ray, at the wheel of his pristine (but ancient) Ford Zephyr (remember them?) we flitted around Manchester city centre in a howling gale looking for some sign of life, never a certain thing to find at 7pm on a Sunday. Eventually as panic began to set in we spotted a lone man in a doorway. Fully kitted for the fray he wore a flat cap, sported half an inch of burning cigarette stuck fast to his bottom lip and clutched a brown paper bag.

'Drunk,' I said to Ray.

'Yes, but he's our only hope,' said Ray, 'Go and ask him.'

So, duly I stepped out of the warmth of the Zephyr and, gale-assisted, half walked and half ran across to the doorway.

'Excuse me, mate,' I chattered, the cold hitting me hard, 'Do you know where Higher Blackley British Legion Club is?'

'No,' came the whisky-fuelled reply. 'But hang on and I'll find out.'

I looked around and there wasn't a soul in sight.

'Hold this,' said the drunk, shoving a brown paper back full of tomatoes in my direction.

With that he set off across the road straight to my car. I thought, 'No!' Oh but, yes! He said to Ray, 'Hey, pal, where are you going?'

'Higher Blackley British Legion.' Said Ray.

'What a stroke of luck,' smiled our friend pointing towards the doorway at me clutching the bag. 'Will you give this poor fellow a lift?' Surely motoring stories don't come odder than that – or do they?

I'd never have thought as a child in bomb-scarred

Bootle that I'd ever have been able to afford a car of any calibre, let alone a new sports car. Nor would I have dreamed I would drive in countries all over the world, left hand side, right hand side but, let me assure you, never both together.

Travel, far and near, develops driving skills but also makes a person aware of traffic problems and odd behaviour from the public at large.

Take Ireland, North and South, and the lovely Irish folk who, as a rule of daily life, will always provide a wee humorous happenstance or two, or three or more, (to be sure, to be sure, to be sure – the reason they have triple yellow lines – Not true! Not true!)

On a fine thoroughfare called O'Connell Street in the fine town of Dublin I personally witnessed a gentle and typically Irish-American exchange. It featured a weather-beaten-faced Dubliner and an American lady burdened down with cameras and guide books. They stood at a pedestrian crossing and the American lass pressed the button to activate it.

After a very short pause, the little green man appeared to indicate a clear crossing. At the same time a loud 'beep-beep' rang through the air.

'What's that noise?' asked the lady as the two crossed the street.

'It's a special sound to warn the blind people,' explained the Dub.

'You mean, they let blind people drive here??'

I bet our Irish friend couldn't wait to pass on that story in the nearest pub – I certainly couldn't.

For those who don't know, O'Connell Street, Dublin is a legendary thoroughfare and in my many sorties to the Emerald Isle I've featured it in song and story – none more frequently told than the classic I picked up at a police function about ten years ago.

Before I begin, you must remember that the Irish police, like the Irish population, have their own way of doing and saying things. A classic from a beat patrolman to a group of teenagers was, 'If you're going to stand there, you'll have to move on!'

But that's not what I was going to tell you. No, my tale is of the man rushing out of a pub towards his car.

'Hey,' bellowed a voice, 'Don't go near that car.'

Turning and seeing a member of the Gardia the fellow said, 'It's all right officer, it's my car. I have the paperwork to prove it.'

'Never mind paperwork,' said the law, 'Don't get into that car.'

'Honestly, officer, I haven't had a drink,' spluttered the motorist.

'Never mind the drink business, don't attempt to get in that car.'

'But, officer … '

'But nothing,' boomed the Gardia,' You obviously don't recognize me, do you? I was in your class at school. You were the most short-sighted boy in our class. You wore huge thick glasses. We used to call you Squinty McGinty. And here you are trying to drive a car without your glasses on!'

'It's different now,' explained McGinty, 'I've got contacts.'

'Listen,' said the policeman,' I don't care who you know, you're not getting in that car without your glasses!' Only in Ireland. Only in Ireland!

A great place for stories old and new. Just ask my managers, Tommy and Kevin.

I was on a tour of Southern Ireland and they had come over on the Liverpool car ferry to join me in the town of Sligo.

On the West coast of the Emerald Isle, Sligo is

reached by road from Dublin following a glorious scenic journey. Today the route is slightly more direct than it was in the days of the story I am about to tell. Then, the motorist would pass through bottleneck towns.

On the old route and after a couple of hours hard driving, they decided to look for an oasis of food and beverage, if only of the caffeinated kind, and quickly spotted a sign saying, 'All day breakfast, two miles!'

Following the arrow the boys turned off left and drove expectantly down an ever-narrowing country lane. Two miles, three miles, four – and still no breakfast. Four and a half and the lane became so narrow that they couldn't have passed a bicycle. Five and a half miles, dead on, and there as if from the mist of Brigadoon, appeared a beautiful cottage bearing a sign, 'All day breakfast.' Eagerly, Tommy and Kevin ploughed into the tasty fare served in mountainous portions. Lovely grub,' said one,' But tell me this. The sign on the main road says you're only two miles down the lane.'

'Sure,' smiled the farmer,' If it had said five and a half you wouldn't have come down.'

And while we're on the subject, take my mate Ted. Ted's a bonny lad. Ex-traffic policeman of serious note, renowned throughout his local constabulary as being somewhat of a tartar where offending motorists were concerned.

'I'll tell you how fearsome he was,' an old workmate assured me, 'If he gave a bloke a breathalyser and it didn't turn green he used to blow in it himself!'

Such a man was my pal, Ted. Keen Northampton town supporter and used car dealer, having a patch near the centre of that fair town. One Saturday afternoon we decided to go to a home match and leave

Ted's number two, a lean and eager lad of twenty, to handle affairs of state for a couple of hours. This he did efficiently and well. 'Too well' thought Ted as we returned in a jarred upstate and scanned the forecourt.

Gone was the Ford Granada Ghia (car of the week) and in its place stood a rusting JCB digger.

'What the (blank) has gone on here?' enquired my pal.

'Sold the Ford for three thousand and took the digger in part-exchange,' smiled the young 'un.

'But the Granada was only two and a half,' spluttered the ex-bobby.

'I know, but I sussed the buyer out and upped the price,' smiled the new apple of Ted's eye, 'And I only allowed him two hundred part chop of the JCB,'

'Good lad,' smiled the gaffer, 'Good lad. You're learning.'Secretly both Ted and I knew the kid had stopped learning. He was teaching now and we were the pupils! But hold hard; that is not where the story ends. Oh no! There's more – a good deal more!

An hour after our return from the football a chap wandered, hands in pockets, into the office and enquired, 'How much would that digger be?'

Sensing a Lincolnshire accent, and guessing correctly that this was a farmer from such parts, Ted replied, 'For yourself would it be, sir?'

'Mebbe, mebbe,' said Mr Prospective Customer.

'Well, a man of your experience could not be kidded I'm sure, sir,' said our man condescendingly. 'I'll give it to you straight. She stands me in at six hundred pounds – cash preferably.'

'Six is about her worth,' nodded Mr Lincoln, 'And six cash it shall be.'

Thus saying, he spat on his right hand and offered it out for Ted to shake. Apparently this is some non-

Liverpool form of invoice and receipt system.

Saying no more the Lincolnshire farmer mounted the iron beast and trundled off into the far beyond leaving us all in a highly elated state; a state, in fact, that only several more pints of Guinness could satisfy. But, whoa, that's still not all. Oh no!

It was my lot to be back in the same sales office of the same used car lot three days later when the phone rang. Ted answered and immediately put the phone on to microphone so I could hear.

'Is that Ted?' came the obvious voice of our Lincoln lad.

'It is.'

'Well, she's acting a bit funny now.'

Obviously it was not his wife, but the JCB he meant.

'When I starts her up in the morning she coughs about six or seven times, splutters a couple of times, coughs again and then very reluctantly kicks into life. What do you think it is?'

'Well,' beamed my pal, 'It sounds as if the warranty's run out.' Ah Ted – you are the one!

Still, that's cars for you. Where there's one there's trouble, even if it is of someone else's making.

Take that classic story of the motorist who returned to find his new Porsche squashed into concertina shape and a total write-off. In his state of stunned disbelief he suddenly spotted a handwritten note lodged under one of the windscreen wipers.

The note read, 'Dear Sir, I'm the bloke who, accidentally reversed his lorry into your car. At the moment there is a crowd of people standing round that thinks I'm leaving my name, address and insurance company – but I'm not!!!'

Shouldn't happen to a dog. But then dogs wouldn't be daft enough to invest in such modes of transport and such bearers of misfortune. I bet you've never met a motorist who claims to have had an incident-free lifetime. Even the experts in buying and selling cars have, in their day, suffered disasters great and small, else how could they have learned to be experts?

But is it worth it? Is all the hassle compensated for by the latest good deal we do or the most recent pleasure trip we take? Of course it is – because the motor car, full of extras like air-conditioning, power-steering, CD player, satellite navigation, is the transport of today.

And today is all that matters. Yesterday is gone forever and tomorrow can look after itself.

Meantime, let me drive, drive, drive today.

Chapter 18

Finally there

So it seems our journey will shortly be over and we shall come to rest having explored most, but not all, means of transportation. And I suppose you 'takes' your choice of which would be the ideal.

For me it must be a mode of transport outside of my control so that I can truly relax and feel the benefits. Maybe for you it is the opposite - maybe being in control is your actual relaxant.

Whatever the choice the options remain many and varied and each in its turn brings humour and wonder into our lives, so that when our travels are finally over we can look back on the memories of places, people and strange happenings. Yes – the memories are all that remain important. And how varied they can be.

I mentioned at the very beginning of this book my recollections of Liverpool's docks and the rows upon rows of beautiful ships that filled every space in every berth. How much romance and fantasy they brought to the mind of the young O'Connor.

How I wished I could but sail on one journey aboard just one of those vessels, to smell the different aromas of cargo, fuel oil, freshly oiled timbers and, most of all, the sea – the sea!

To drift in the darkness of a transatlantic night and drink brandy from a huge glass, take puffs of a huge cigar and listen, captivatingly, to the life story of the crew and the other passengers.

Yes, that was my ambition if I ever won the pools; to be one of a very select band of passengers to travel across the world on a merchantman and become a man of mystery and experience whose life and movements would be as the rhythm of the slow and steady throbbing motion of the powerful engines.

Oh to fall asleep at night and awaken to the sound of anchors dropping and the ship berthing; or to feel the vibrations of the engine as the ship kicks from stillness to life and prepares to leave a foreign port at night – lit only by the harbour lights and the ever-watching moon. Was there ever a more thrilling prospect?

I do it all now as part of my work and I should really have become attuned and blasé. But no, the feeling of wonder is still there, I'm happy to say.

So ships and the sea loom large in my thoughts when I think of travel. Mystery is all-important to me, but so too is humour. Nowhere, surely is humour more apparent as when talking of moving people from A to B.

Take simple things like the alternate view of the Tour de France bicycle endurance race. As one observer said to his pal, 'Why do those blokes on the telly go through all that pain and stress, cycling mile after mile, day after day, up hills and down, in the most horrendous conditions? It's absolute torture.'

'Well,' explained his friend, 'The winner gets half a million dollars.'

'Yes,' said the first, 'But why do the others do it?'

Often, for a good funny story a machine isn't ever necessary. Shanks' pony is sometimes sufficient. Like the attractive young lady who, one summer's day, decided to disrobe and partake of that most modern of sports – streaking!

Having caused chaos by trotting along the clockwise carriageway of the 25 motorway, and being pursued hotfoot (literally) by two members of the constabulary she ran up the embankment, through a field and through a building site. To check her directions for escape she called to a bricklayer,

'Am I all right for Chorley Wood?'

'Not 'arf!' he replied, 'Chorley – look who's here to see you!!'

No matter how we travel and no matter where we do it, there are always characters to be met, experiences to savour and tales to bring home.

For years Ireland bore the mantle of home of the odd and unusual. Ask any Amercian tourist who ever visited the country and they will have something unusual to tell – like the Texan on a visit to Dublin who found a stall selling skulls and relics of the dead and gone.

'This one, sir, is the actual skull of the late and great Saint Patrick, Patron of Ireland and the holies of the holies,' said the stall holder, 'And it's yours for only £500.'

'A bargain,' thought Tex and paid up and was happy.

Three years later he returned for another holiday and decided to seek further relics to buy, the first having been a great topic of conversation.

'Well, sir,' began Murphy the stallkeeper, little realizing he had a repeat customer, 'This small skull is the actual skull of the late Saint Patrick …'

'It can't be,' said the yank, 'I bought that on my last trip and it was a lot larger than this one!'

'Ah – that's because, you see,' replied the quick-thinking Murphy, 'This was his skull when he was only a boy!'

OK, with stories like that Ireland gained a reputation, but what about Scotland? Home of Rabbie Burns, Robert the Bruce and Billy Evans – Billy Evans? Billy Evans? How did he get in here?

Well, Billy's an Edinburgh taxi driver who delights in leading passengers a merry dance. Sad, or perhaps glad, to say he caught me with a beauty; one of those old but gold yarns that would have seemed to happen to everyone else, but that you are never warned about.

The bold Billy was driving me from the airport to a city centre hotel. The sun had set and the rush hour was over as we proceeded almost sedately with Mr Evans saying next to nothing except, 'My brother drives a cab as well, you know.'

'Really?' said I.

'Shouldn't, though, with his problem.'

'Problem?'

'Ay – he's colour blind or something. He stops at green lights and goes at red.'

'Wow,' I gasped, 'That's seriously dangerous – almost homicidal.'

'Ay – it's bad right enough. Shouldn't be on the road.'

So saying Billy came upon green traffic lights and screeched to a halt.

'Why are you stopping on green?' I said.

'Well, you never know – my brother could be coming the other way!!'

Caught again. No apologies. Sucker of the year; but, at least, a story to tell.

And after all, isn't that one of the pre-requisites of a traveler - the ability to laugh at everything including our own shortcomings? Yes – it's a grand life when you know what you're doing, where you're going and all, or most, of the pitfalls that await you.

On other pages I've listed the dos and don'ts of getting about. Good directions, good fodder, the right clothing, the right company. And all in their own way are vital ingredients. But surely the greatest element, the little bit of magic that enhances any journey is what we ourselves put into it.

Like the great Oscar Wilde visiting America, who noticed a question on the customs form, asking, 'Do you plan to overthrow the government of the United States?'

To which Oscar wrote the answer, 'Sole purpose of visit!'

Yes – that's what's needed. A slice of humour, mental effort as well as physical. The attempt to leave behind in distant places a little of ourselves, just as we take home a little of them.

So, dear reader, wherever you go – go safe, go sure, but most importantly go in peace and happiness – because the coming back will be all the more joyful.